TRAGEDY'S ARK

A Book of Comfort for Disheartened Parents

Jayne Garrison

BALBOA.
PRESS
A DIVISION OF HAY HOUSE

Balboa Press books may be ordered through booksellers or by contacting:
Balboa Press
A Division of Hay House
1663 Liberty Drive
Bloomington, IN 47403
www.balboapress.com
1-(877) 407-4847

ISBN: 978-1-4525-3748-1 (sc)
ISBN: 978-1-4525-3747-4 (e)
ISBN: 978-1-4525-3749-8 (hc)
Library of Congress Control Number: 2011914396

"Scripture taken from the Holy Bible, New International Version, copyright 1973,1978, and
1984 by International Bible Society. Used by permission of Zondervon Bible Publishers."

This book is not intended as a substitute for professional counseling—neither spiritual nor psychological,
but as an inspirational lift. All information is based on personal insight and on the belief that
God's unlimited love overcomes and conquers all. The third person pronouns (he and she) are used
interchangeably for readability, and are not intended to classify any one behavior to a specific gender.

Printed in the United States of America
Balboa Press rev. date: 11/09/2011

Also by Jayne Garrison

The ABCs of Christian Mothering
The Christian Working Mother's Handbook
The A–to–Z Guide for New Mothers
The Working Mom's Survival Guide
Living With the Challenging Child

For
Olie

About the Cover

The cover is a picture by the author's husband, Olie Garrison, taken inside the Painted Church, Honaunau, Hawaii.

Preface

When my youngest daughter left home for the arms of a nationally-known street gang, her father and I began a seven-year prayer vigil for her safe return. That she did eventually return to us was not as surprising as what she returned home to—unconditional love that had not only restored our family but changed us into a "different" kind of people who saw with deeper eyes and thought with wider minds. This book is a collection of the truth lessons we learned on our pathway to peace.

What Others Say About Tragedy's Ark

"Jayne Garrison is a great writer, and I am impressed with the depth of her work. Never is there a time when parents feel more hopeless than when their child is on the edge of a cliff of drugs, alcohol or crime. Parents are in a panic—without a clue as to where to turn, or who to ask for help. I have personally witnessed parents searching for answers on what will save their child and their relationship with him in time. Ms. Garrison offers from her personal experience, a path to success in an enjoyable, short, to the point read on getting through each day, and getting through the crisis.
 I recommend this book."

-Christopher Ian Chenoweth, www.positiveChristianity.org

"Tragedy's Ark is a wonderful source of comfort and wisdom for hurting parents, written by someone who truly understands. The easy-to-read format makes it a win-win selection for anyone undergoing a personal, family crisis."

-Laura Silva Quesada, President, Silva International

Table of Contents

CHAPTER 1

Smile - Maybe He Isn't Calling From Jail

Keep the faith.
Stay upbeat.
Smile.
Be happy.
Be Kind.
Count your blessings.
Never give up.
It could be worse.

You've heard these words a million times, but never were they more unwelcome than now, as you sit at the kitchen table mulling over your child's latest disaster. Typically, there's no need putting a name to the crisis—they are always different, each one seeming a little more problematic than its predecessor. John has been arrested for stealing. You've just come home from the police station. Tiffany has been using the latest fad drug. You were the one who found her stash. Lonnie has posed for pornographic photos which were somehow discovered by the law. You're scared to answer the phone. Cory has been expelled from school for carrying a gun in his backpack. Plans for graduation with a scholarship have flown out the window. Sunny has pushed the results of a pregnancy test in front of you. It's positive. Chad has hesitantly revealed his sexual preference. There's no way you can tell his father.

Tristan has been arrested. They think he killed someone, and you're afraid he might have. It is, in fact, this "fear" that seems to be the underlying factor in all your emotions these days.

"The older Todd gets, the less we can do to undo the damage; or to protect him from himself. The stakes get higher," one father confided in a moment of sorrowful stress.

How well you understand.

On the other hand, your situation may not be at all so dramatic. Maybe you're simply dealing with Jason who lies, or Katy who refuses to come home at curfew. Perhaps it's Allison, who blatantly cheats on exams, or Damien who sneaks out of the house at night to smoke with friends. It could even be that you're struggling with 42-year-old Greg who won't get a job, and insists upon living with you, or 50-year-old Margie whose drug problems have taken the family on a series of roller coaster rides for the past 30 years. Perhaps it's just the overwhelming sadness of being a parent to a grown child who no longer wants to share his life or the joy of his children with you.

Whatever your particular problem is, the fact of the matter remains that something went terribly wrong in your family dynamics, and you're not sure what or how it occurred. Until now, you've equated problem children with bad parenting. But suddenly, you're confused. You don't see yourself as such a bad parent. As far as you know, you've never been unloving, uncaring or unfit. You feel pretty sure that you taught the right values--- and you know for a fact that you've had your child in church and held him in your prayers right next to your heart. At the same time, moments like this make your ego look around for an event or a person to blame, and with society telling us that "it's all caused by something Mom and Dad didn't or did do," this little part of you pushes itself to the forefront to be cleared of all fault. You immediately start to examine every little action---every little nuance of your parenting life--- for the culprit of your problem, but quickly discover that it's impossible for you to remember just what kind of a parent you really have been.

You're no longer sure if you were truly strong, authoritative, and unyielding in the things that mattered. You're no longer sure if you touched enough, praised when appropriate or listened with both ears. You wonder if you disciplined correctly---were not too lax or too strict. Even when you suspect that someone else such as the school is at fault, you wonder what you could have done or said that would have made a difference.

And how about God? Where was he in all of this you want to know? Better yet, where is he now? Suddenly your thinking becomes a kaleidoscope of contradictions, and you begin toying with the idea that perhaps God could have made things turn out differently if only you <u>had</u> been the right kind of parent---the kind of parent he wanted you to be. Whatever that was. If only he had loved you as much as you thought he did. If only you had been lovable enough for him to favor you with his love.

Your mind rocks with emotions so varied, you don't know what to address first. Should you try to curb your anger? Seek comfort for your hurt? Try counseling for your fears? Concentrate on good health habits to remedy your stress? Look for deeper religion in a different church? How can you possibly know what to do next, when your child seems to have destroyed both his life and yours with a single thoughtless act carrying unredeemable consequences?

Now take a deep breath and as you exhale, allow yourself to envision all these troubling thoughts leaving you with exhalation. The picture is not as formidable as you may have thought, because life is not always what it seems. Ironically, though most of us intellectually acknowledge this statement as true, few of us take the time to examine life events with the kind of questions that would enable us to prove it so. Perhaps this is because, stepping outside of the comfortably "known" requires us not only to think differently, but to see differently and act differently. It asks us to question the status quo—maybe even challenge religious and social dogmas that have been in place and served as a guiding light throughout the ages of man.

Yet, when we do choose to view life through this different perspective and agree to let go of at least a few of those long-formed opinions, life becomes less threatening, less nonsensical and easier to live. What's more, we find ourselves privileged to take part in a new spiritual drama, unfolding not in churches or other religious arenas, but in the heart of the human family itself. Remarkably, we are allowed to see that the essence of truth Jesus spoke about in the Bible was not in "thinking new thoughts," "fighting spiritual demons," or even in "performing spectacular miracles." In the end, when all was said and done, Jesus surprised his followers with a truth, that while famously profound, was also so simple in concept, that it is uniformly overlooked in favor of more complicated, high-sounding theology. The essence of this powerful truth is love.

The directions for finding your way to this truth and making it work for you are easily stated. See only with the eyes of love. Speak only with the voice of love. Act only in the ways of love. When we follow these tenets, the situation that now causes you to sit at the table with your head in your hands stops being a tragedy and becomes an opportunity to do what you were created to do; what you have been commanded to do; what you know how to do, whether you realize it now or not---and that is love. More than blame, more than criticism, more than judgment and certainly more than anger---this is a moment that needs your love.

Perhaps you think I'm making light of a very serious problem in your life, and that this is not what you needed to hear right now. If so, let me assure you, I have sat in your seat at that very table of despair. I *know* what you're feeling, but I happen to have encouraging news. I have discovered that Jesus comes to us in these human moments, where it is often easier to see him than it is in the perfect ones. Perhaps this is because, from the beginning, God came down to our human level to teach us about love. He introduced his child to the world in a human form we would recognize and understand---a child who would bring dramatic changes to the human family at large. Children are like that. They force us to change through learning and loving, and this is what can happen to you now.

No, it's not the life you once dreamed of. So far, your parenting experience has been like a vacation gone bad. Instead of the happy, picture-perfect postcard memories, you've been left with the flat tires and wrong turns. It's not where you wanted to go. But sometimes God brings us to places we don't want to be in order to teach us the lesson we are supposed to learn.

I ask you to step back and look again at the situation in front of you, but this time, from a different perspective. Instead of feeling unfairly attacked, consider yourself special---consider yourself loved--- you have just been handed proof that God is not through with you, yet. He has come to you through your child with the promise of your personal growth. He's not telling you to solve the problem, or change the scenario. That part is in his hands and under his complete control. He is simply challenging you to love.

So, it is in keeping with this challenge, that I offer a collection of positive ideas shared in the spirit of love. Think of them as ideas to ponder, to re-work, to try out, and finally, to make your own. I want you to be comfortable with the fact that this isn't a book that has to be read front to back, but one that may be worked through at any pace that feels good, starting on any page that seems right. It's been said that the deepest connection between people is the recognition of mutual knowledge---an inner knowing of what the other person is going through. As you consider each idea presented here, remember that you and I are "knowing" friends, and my love follows you with support on the journey ahead.

> My soul glorifies the Lord and my spirit rejoices in God my Savior,
>   for he has been mindful of the humble state of his servant.
>
> Luke 1:46-48

CHAPTER 2

If I'm Here, Where is God?

A PRAYER (Well, Sort of)

Listen to me, God, if you are out there—Listen to me. Are you there?
I think I am going to die. I think this moment is too horrible—too
traumatic—too hostile—too cold for anyone to "make it" through.
I think I am living a nightmare that I will never wake up from.

What you want to know: Will I survive? Is God there for me?

What you need to know: Yes on both counts. The truth is that God is always with us, and no matter how much this moment may feel like the end of the world, it's not. The clock keeps ticking and the world spins on. But, you may *feel* as if you can't live through it. Your chest feels so tight that you have to catch your breath, while your stomach is twisted into knots of turmoil that cause you to rock back and forth as if riding in a small boat on dangerous waters. In one swift action, your child has toppled the world you know. Yet, here you are, still alive and going nowhere.

So, why do you feel so physically defeated? Perhaps because of the nature of the experience. Depending upon its severity, a family crisis comes at you like a personal tsunami. The ugly news is delivered to you with a hit of energy that may literally knock the breath out of you. For a moment, you feel "pulled under" by the force of the giant wave, and you wonder if you'll ever be able to "come up for air." In reality, the bad news *is* energy. Imagine little bits and pieces of negativity coming together until it forms a big, black ball heading straight for you. This is the force that affects you so strongly. However, it need not overcome you. You can block its power from penetrating your psyche by learning to stay in the present moment.

Yes, it's a buzz cliché—a trendy sounding phrase that doesn't mean a thing—until put into action. It's something we hear a lot about, but seldom act on, because we're not sure how or where to begin. We may not even be sure that it's truly possible, given our state of distress. That's okay, perfectly normal and, more common than not. Nevertheless, just for now, try to be trusting, try to relax and lean into the moment. I am about to tell you exactly how to stay there, and it's easy.

For starters, it often helps to go within and center yourself first with prayer and meditation. In a moment of crisis, this may be nothing more than asking God for help and then, focusing on your breathing with a series of long inhalations followed by slow exhalations. Staying in the present is concentrating on the now. It's not going over what has just happened or worrying about what might occur in the future, because the present has no beginning and no ending. This is not a new idea to most of us, but putting it into practice is not often accomplished, because we simply don't put effort into exploring this space.

If you are having trouble with the concept of now, try describing what you are feeling this very minute. Write it down. You will probably find that this simple exercise is very revealing as to what the present actually is. With few exceptions such as physical pain or terror---the present is not usually as unbearable as we think. It just is, and you just are--- within it.

About Prayer

It certainly is all right to speak your mind to God. If anything, this displays a profound belief in his very existence. However, it is important to learn to thank God for at least one thing every day. Gratitude multiplies goodness. This is a law of the universe that simply has to be learned. For now, while things are difficult, stick to the basics. You don't have to pretend that everything horrible is good---just find that one little thing out there that's not so bad. Today, it could be this minute.

Pray With Me Now

Thank you, God, for this minute in time.
I am breathing.
My blood is circulating.
I am allowing my mind to empty itself of thought.
Right this minute, I can honestly say that
nothing bad is happening.
It's just you and me, God.
So, this minute is precious,
and
I thank you for it.
Amen

*Hint: Watch your pets. They will teach you how to live in the present. Study nature. It, too, will show you how to "be." There is something sacred and precious about the moment at hand because it truly is God's gift to us. This tiny increment of time is what belongs to us—what we can be sure about. Everything else is an unknown. Enjoy your gift, and savor it as proof that God is indeed, "out there."

"Who of you by worrying can add a single hour to his life?"

Matthew 6:27

CHAPTER 3

Blueprint for Comfort

A PRAYER

Dear God
What am I supposed to do?
I'm praying but I don't feel especially loving.
I feel angry and hurt.
Don't you know a stiff upper lip is only for kewpie dolls?
How am I suppose to focus on love
when I can barely put one foot in front of the other?

What you want to know: What is something real that I can do right now to make myself feel like going on?

What you need to know: Use soothing methods for heart-breaking conditions. Remember that the body is a sensitive machine. Yelling, quarrelling and worrying will eventually reward you with nothing more than health problems. Replace these reactions with a soothing plan of action. Build an ark—figuratively speaking, of course.

In the Bible story of Noah and the Ark, God instructed Noah to build the ark *before* the flood. The detailed instructions given to him became Noah's plan of action. The actual ark was his refuge once the storm hit. This is what you will be doing---building an atmosphere of soothing refuge to rest in during stormy times. Think of it as your emotional ark.

Building inner strength with scripture and sound thinking has always been a good way to prepare for difficult times. You may have even heard of such activity referred to as a type of "ark" building. However, in this instance, you will be carrying the idea a step further by constructing an actual physical environment.

Spend a few minutes now, laying the ground work for your plan of action. Begin by thinking about what makes you feel good. Include the names of people you like to talk to, places you like to visit, foods you like to cook and activities you like to partake in. Write your choices in a notebook that you can consult when a crisis leaves you too frazzled to think.

Unlike Noah's ark, there are no particular specifications for an emotional ark, though I can highly recommend building one from a box. Here's a fun project designed to take your mind off the issue at hand and allow you to get lost in the present, which is one good way of finding at least temporary peace of mind.

Directions for Building an Emotional Ark

Locate a beautiful, medium sized box. Hobby stores offer moderately priced small, wooden chests and lovely cardboard hat boxes---either of which would work well. You can also decorate any cardboard box with attractive wrapping or wall paper.

ITEMS TO PLACE IN YOUR BOX
➢ A good quality fleece blanket
➢ A soothing CD
➢ A stash of healthy food that stores well. Perhaps a can of cashews or a can of your favorite soup and a box of crackers
➢ A book that you like to read and re-read
➢ A bar of expensive soap for a nice, hot soak in the bath
➢ A craft project that you know you will enjoy
➢ A DVD (preferably a comedy that will make you laugh)

Keep your box in an easily accessible place and check it now and then to update it with your latest interests. When a crisis does hit, turn off the television first, so that the "quiet" of the house can begin to help heal your hurt. Take stock of your surroundings, cleaning up clutter that will only add to chaotic thinking, go for a walk to work off excessive anger or to simply release energy, and prepare one of the comfort foods that you've set aside for this purpose. Finally, retreat to your ark and shut the door behind you.

There are no hard and fast rules as to how long you should stay in your ark, though the size of your box and the nature of your ark plan will naturally limit you to a fairly temporary visit. As he did with Noah, God will send a sign when it's time to come out and face the world again, (though it probably will not be a dove.) Suddenly, you will just "know" that you have what it takes to meet the challenge in front of you. Your fear and despair will have been replaced with renewed wisdom and enhanced inner strength, giving you the resolve and determination to step forth. God bless you. You most certainly will be all right. This problem will move into the best possible outcome. Your personal growth will take place on many different levels. You and your child and your family and all the people you encounter as you work through the problem will be irrevocably changed for the better. But as for the ark—the one that you built according to your own private needs—the one you ran to for comfort and healing when the bottom fell out of your world—it remains on top of the mountain, waiting to be used the next time around.

Pray with me now

Dear God,
Thank you for wrapping me in a cocoon of your love
and
placing me in the ark.
Amen

Affirmation: God has a plan for my life, and I accept it with love.

CHAPTER 4

Who's to Blame?

A PRAYER

Dear Father,
I only want to know what I did wrong with this child.
What part of this did I do wrong?
or
don't you care?

> What you are asking: Is this my fault? Does God care about me?

> What you need to know: It's not a matter of placing blame. God cares more about you than he does determining the cause and effect of events.

Unless you were an abusive or neglectful parent (and it's highly unlikely you'd be reading this book in that situation), this recent calamity is not your fault. Influenced by our culture, your child has simply made an unwise choice. Now is the time to realize you are not your child. Certainly, you were the vessel for his entry into this world, and certainly, it was your job to get him off to the best possible start, but he is his own person with his own divine mission to fulfill. Even when guidance and discipline still fall within our parenting boundaries, as long as we have equipped him with the tools to make the right choices, we are not responsible for his wrong ones.

Of course, some of the people who love you most will point fingers at you with well-meaning accusations. "If only you had been such and such. If only you had done this, instead of that. If only you had gone here instead of there."

Bear in mind that even when you suspect they may be right, you did the best you knew how to do at the time. Remember this is a growing journey. And no matter what happened in the past, it can be recognized as an important life passage. The past has been a good teacher. If there is, in fact, remorse on your part at this point, it's simply because you have now arrived at a place of deeper understanding and stronger capabilities. Use this understanding and more experienced viewpoint to love yourself—even as you reach out with love for your child.

Does God care about you? You bet! God is always present, always loving, always the truth, even in bad times. Remember, the challenge in front of you is not some form of punishment, but simply an experience. God stays with you throughout this experience whether you want him there or not, but when we connect through prayer and awareness of his presence, we are endowed with his power and strength.

Pray With Me Now

Father God
Thank you for trusting me with
the challenge of my life.
Even though I may not always feel up to the fight,
I know I can do the job
with your strength
with your power
and
with your love.
Amen

Thought for the day: Everything that happened in the past prepares me for taking right action.

CHAPTER 5

About Those Other Lovely Parents

A PRAYER

Dear God,
The conversation has turned to children,
And I'm not talking.
The room is a bee hive of noise—each voice raising louder than the other.
They are boasting of their children's accomplishments, God. And I am silent.
They are boasting of their children's virtues, God. And I say nothing.
They are boasting of innocent, young lives going forth in purity and goodness.
And I am quiet.
It's not just the matter of being overwhelmed by too many women---I have
nothing to say.
And I want to leave.
But since there is no graceful exit, help me to endure.

What you are asking: How do I gracefully handle bragging parents, when my heart is breaking?

What you need to know: Your hurt feelings are justified, but you are greater than these feelings and can handle the situation with grace and dignity.

People don't perceive problem children in quite the same manner they do other types of family crisis. The death of a loved one, the loss of a job, a financial or natural disaster all elicit some degree of sympathy. When people are around others undergoing any of these traumas, they will usually watch their manners. For instance, people won't usually flaunt success in the face of a friend's financial catastrophe, or talk about children in the presence of a couple grieving the death of a child. Most people will even hold back on celebratory remarks about a job promotion in front of a friend who has just lost a job, and few people would invite the survivors of an environmental disaster to view the latest decorating accomplishment of their own home. At the same time, there is no avoiding or tip-toeing around the subject of children in front of the parents of a struggling child.

When we visit the parents of successful children, we must listen courteously to the long litany of Paul's athletic prowess, look at Lisa's cheerleading pictures, touch Cara's dance trophy. Grades, popularity and appearance are all discussed and held out for our what? Approval? Acknowledgement? Envy?

If you find yourself in this situation, don't try to make sense out of what God has done to your life---be generous, and give your approval to whatever brash matter is being placed in front of you. You don't need those things to make you happy. Your life is in God's will, and when we are accepting of his will, what he has given us is all that's necessary. What we don't have is of no use to us.

God's will for our life is a private matter; whatever lessons that come with it are for us alone. Likewise, God has words that are for us alone, and sometimes these words are heard through suffering. Don't worry about what other people are talking about—just concentrate on hearing what God is saying to you. While other parents are bragging about their children, God is telling you that he loves you, and that you are always an important member of his family.

A practical hint: When people do ask you about your child, you think they are really concerned, and so you honor this concern. You probably stammer out a jumble of words about his latest catastrophe, and what you are doing to amend it. There is usually an embarrassed hush throughout the crowd, followed by someone jumping in quickly with more good news about her child. Happily, you don't have to be victimized in this way.

Instead of "telling all," learn to speak only the highest thoughts about your child. Believe me, it will take some practice and perhaps even preparation, but it can be accomplished by having "stock" answers to the usual questions on hand.

> For example:
> "How is _____doing now?"
> Your answer: "Just great!"
> "But what is he doing now?"
> Your answer: "Oh, my goodness, I can't even keep up with it anymore."
> "Wasn't he in prison?" or "Did he ever graduate?" or "Did he ever get off drugs?"
> Your answer: "Listen, nothing keeps that kid down. He is so resilient. And we are so proud of him!"

Remember to always include the word "proud" in there somewhere—even if you don't really feel it. The more you say it, the closer you come to feeling it. Besides, it's hard to come back with a hurtful statement when a parent expresses pride.

Pray With Me Now

Dear Heavenly Father
Thank you for helping me see that
my happiness
does not depend upon equal "footing" with others,
but in being in the right and perfect place in life to know your love.
For this love, I thank you.
Amen

CHAPTER 6

When It Hurts So Bad

A PRAYER

Oh, God, look at me.

I am standing in the dining room putting the finishing touches on a lavish holiday tea table, but my mind is clearly not on the festivities at hand. My 18-year-old child has just shattered the mood with news of his recent arrest. To our God-fearing, law-abiding family the news is like being hit below the belt with a baseball bat. No one in our family has ever even been arrested much less spent the night in jail.

I feel so angry, God. I feel so violated and scared. In uncharacteristic clumsiness, I topple a candle stick that sends a glass of water spilling across the table.

God, I know this arrest is not my fault. I know that you love me and care about me. I know that you still love my child.

But so what?

It still hurts.

Tell me how to make it stop hurting.

What you want to know: If I'm not to blame, why does it hurt? What will make it stop hurting?

What you need to know: Pain hurts, but it eventually wears off.

We hurt for a myriad of reasons. For one thing, we are disappointed. Our child has let us down again, and it hurts. We hurt for the child because we know how scary the legal system can be for a youngster, and we know how harsh criminal justice can be. But most of all, we hurt because this child, whom we love so much, simply can't seem to choose right. We ache for him. It seems unfair; it seems unkind, (particularly when we have prayed and prayed for divine intervention); it seems unthinkable that God will not reach out and rescue this troubled spirit.

We accept that nothing happens to us except by the will of God, and yet, we practically curse this moment of anguish, because we don't understand. God's will must conform to our limited realm of understanding and come in forms that we can recognize as good. How dare God use any unpleasant approach to produce his will. How can he use the mistreatment of my child? My own ostracism from the community? The financial downfall of my family? The poor health of someone I love?

When these feelings and questions arise, it's important to know that God's will isn't limited to the good and grand. He is free to use everything necessary to accomplish his goal. When we know this, we can know there is God-given justice in all events; we just can't always see it at the moment. Understand that when your child suffers from the hand of others or from his own seeming inability to choose right, there is learning for everyone involved. Your child grows stronger and more knowledgeable. You learn patience, forgiveness and love. His avenger, should there be one, is given the opportunity for personal growth that may go beyond anything we can imagine. This may not make sense if you see it happen over and over without evidence of change taking place, but growing and learning for all people takes many forms. Though growth may not occur as a direct result of the incident at hand, remember that people are often able to align various incidents into a pattern that leads to eventual enlightenment.

God's justice is justice with a purpose. Instead of feeling sorry for your child's inability to make right decisions, realize that even this is part of God's plan---a plan that was likely agreed upon before your child came to earth. Realize that as such, you and your child are not alone. One colorful Bible "celebrity" who lived a life directed by God's justice was Samson, whom you probably remember from the story of Samson and Delilah. Take time to re-read this story in Judges 13. Though Samson's life was riddled with the torment of wrong choices, God's plan depended upon Samson being the person he was. We're told that his parents knew from the beginning that Samson was a special child, but we don't know just how much they knew or understood as to how it would all play out. Chances are good that their son's unusual behavior kept them in a fairly heartbroken state. They couldn't have possibly foreseen his historical spot in Biblical history. You and I, on the other hand, can let go of the pain that comes with raising a difficult child, and replace it with the comfort of knowing that there is divine justice in God's plan.

As for the other kind of justice—that getting even—getting what you deserve kind of feeling---justice will prevail. Someday there will be justice for all the wrong done against your child, as well as justice for all that your child has done to wrong others. It just might be a wash with both parties coming to the realization of their action. Or perhaps it will be a moment of recognition when each party suddenly sees the Christ in the other. What sweet justice we can envision on that day. But for now, all that matters is remembering that the existence of spiritual justice provides us with the opportunity to find blessings and advantages in even the most painful experience. We are free to watch the unfolding in a relaxed state of grace, because, after all, we know that God's justice will someday bring our child to a good place.

Pray With Me Now

Dear God
Thank you for spiritual justice
even when I don't understand how it can possibly be.
Just knowing that spiritual justice is a part of your plan,
enables me to see a glimpse of your healing love,
and the pain is a little less.
Amen

Affirmation: When my child doesn't choose right action, I am reminded he is part of a greater plan that I can't see.

Practical action to take: When we hurt, we long to be comforted, but often there's no one around to do the job. We can do this for ourselves by entering the kingdom of God. For if the Kingdom of God is within, then somewhere within the gates of the kingdom, we will no doubt be able to locate not just the "child within," but the Christ Child within. We can call forth the Christ Child within and nurture him with love. Here is how this works. Begin by visualizing the image of the infant Jesus. See yourself pick him up and hold him. Allow yourself to actually feel this taking place. You are now holding the Christ Child within, and everything you would do for a human child can be done for the Christ Child within you. Love him. Nurture him. Sing to him. Play with him—all in your mind's eye. Next, feed the child by taking time to pray. Feed him by acknowledging his gifts, by reading wholesome material, and by recognizing God. In fact, thank God now for bringing this child into your life and thank the child for being awake and receptive to your love. The Christ Child within is never demanding, and always ready to receive, no matter the circumstance, because he knows only love. Best of all, spending time with the Christ Child within is a way of reconnecting to our inner strength in times of fragility.

CHAPTER 7

Let Go and Let God

A PRAYER

Dear God,
People are always telling me to release my child.
I've tried, God.
It doesn't seem to work.
How can I possibly fully and freely release him?
I love him too much.

What you want to know: Will releasing my child help? Is it really possible to let him "go?"

What you need to know: Letting go is an important part of healing and growing for both you and your child.

The idea is certainly nothing new. Probably all of us, at one time or another has vowed to let our child go his way, usually after some well-meaning person tells us we need to.

"I'm releasing him---letting him go," we announce to our friends.

And we do---for a few minutes. But it isn't long before the doubts and fears begin to overwhelm us, and we can't resist worrying and fretting once again.

"I can't release someone whom I love so much and have prayed for for so long," you may find yourself complaining.

Don't be so sure. You *can* release and let go, because it's not the person you're releasing, but the situation surrounding him and the feelings inside of you. When you look at it this way, you'll be amazed at how successfully you let go.

A few situations and feelings that you can think about releasing are:

Preconceived Expectations

Vow to stop making preconceived expectations for your child. While they may feel like *your* dreams, conceived with the best interest of your child in mind, they are really determined by people who don't even know him—society at large. Not to mention that such expectations seldom have anything to do with God's plan for him. Whenever these inappropriate hopes and desires for your child do surface in your mind, you can give up the sensation of feeling disgruntled and unhappy, by remembering to say to yourself, "That's not a part of God's plan for _____, and I don't need it to feel good about being his parent."

The Need to Control

Give up the belief that "Mother knows best." Maybe there was an element of truth to the statement when your child was younger, but now is the time to reconsider those thoughts. There may, in fact, be occasions when your child's way is best for him, or when you are simply wrong and he is right. Acknowledge that there is much that the older child has to learn for himself, and that we all reach an age when our parents are no longer the teachers. One way to do this is to try to remember what you learned from your mother from the age of 18 on. Chances are you'll draw a blank. It's just that because our difficult children are usually immature and most often still at home, it's easy to think of them as little children rather than young adults. Give up your craving for control and start looking for those things that your child is teaching you.

The Desire to Fix the Problem

Stop trying to be the "fixer upper." It's a surprising fact to many of us, but we are not responsible for making our child's life work. Only he can take the necessary steps to walk in the right direction. When we try to clean up his messes and make all the efforts necessary for improvement, our child gains nothing, and he certainly doesn't change. Let go of the need to fix the problem and allow the child to learn whatever skills God intends for him to master through self-actualization. When we let go of the desire to "save" our child, we are finally admitting that only our child can save himself.

Feelings of Anger and Resentment

Let go of damaging anger. It may seem that your child has caused you grief on purpose, or at the very least has been nothing but inconsiderate and thoughtless. It's normal to feel angry or resentful in these circumstances, but these feelings won't serve you in any helpful way. Nor will they change things for the better. When angry thoughts overtake you, try writing a statement of love for your child 15 times. Do it throughout the day, as many times as necessary. Get away from the scene of disturbance, and surround yourself with peaceful, loving friends, or create a peaceful, loving sanctuary with your emotional ark. Give up anger in favor of love.

What Could Have Been

Give up the non-existent past—the one that never happened. The saddest part of parenting a difficult child is the sense of loss. At some point, we are sure to look back on the past with regret. We regret that we didn't ever have a close relationship with this child during his growing-up years. We regret that he never was able to make friends with the right kind of people, that he never studied, or graduated from high school. We regret, regret, regret.

Stop it. Your child has had the perfect, God-intended life up to now. Perhaps things will change at some point on the time line, but only when the child is ready for growth. Pull up all the good memories you have and begin to write them in a journal. As you remember, try to recall the humorous touches to the story —the time your child was making cookies and turned the mixer on so high that it shot dough onto the ceiling---the time your child wore almost every article of clothing that he owned to school---the time he got a speeding ticket on the way to pay for an earlier one. These are the moments life is made up of—and the kind of memories that help us move beyond what could have been into now.

What Not to Give Up

Never stop loving your child, and never stop praying for him. God doesn't ever tell us we should give up hope or love. They are his gifts to us, and will be our greatest source of strength whatever the situation or emotion in front of us.

Pray With Me Now

Dear Father
Thank you for giving me the freedom of release.
I know that when I release my human perceptions of the perfect life,
I give myself and my child the gift of grace,
and we are able to rest in the arms of your love
while you do the work.
For such sweet freedom, I thank you again.
Amen

Thought for the Day: A popular saying reminds us that God hasn't quit and put us in charge! He is still very much in control, so there's no use in trying to do it all by yourself.

Chapter 8

Judge Not

A PRAYER

Dear God,
I am lying in bed counting the chimes on the anniversary clock, listening for the sound of my child's car.
Midnight
One o'clock
Two o'clock
Three
Time ticks on.
Finally, I hear the key turn in the door, and I am both happy and angry at once.

Part of me wants to confront him—to see for myself if he has been drinking or looks sexually tousled. The other part of me backs down and rolls over; satisfied that he is at least safely home. But my mind doesn't rest. I imagine what he may have been doing---where he was and who he may have been with. The pictures parading before my mind's eye are ugly and dirty.

I pray for a healing, God. Lord, I beg you; rid my child of his filthy mind— his disgusting habits---his scumbag behavior—or, dare I say, his unclean spirit?

I ask you to make him more like me—good, upright and...spiritually clean. You know what I mean, God?

What you are asking: Why is my child living this life I don't understand? Why isn't he of higher moral character? Why doesn't God act to change this situation NOW?

What you need to know: Perhaps we are asking the wrong questions. Maybe we should be asking this: Who is more "unclean?" The person committing the act? Or the person judgmentally obsessing about the act?

When our children do something against our own moral code, and we are angry to the point of having an unforgiving spirit, we are probably basing our feelings on fear. Going against moral laws carries real-life consequences and none of them are good. But chances are, you have discussed these fears with your child in such a way that he could have seen the truth if he had wanted to. And chances are, you have asked God to intervene, and he hasn't in the way you could imagine. If God is not tied up in knots over our child's moral faux pas during this learning phase, should we be?

God wants our thoughts to be healing thoughts of light and love, but when we are obsessed by our child's deviant lifestyle—the obsession controls our mind with the baser side of consciousness, and we are unable to reach this light and love. We become the one with the unclean spirit, so to speak. If we think something we can do or say will bring about a healing, we are the one seeking satisfaction from the flesh. When our obsession with our child's behavior causes us to rant and rave---we are the one resisting truth.

However, whatever our "unclean" spirit may be, (and you can be sure, it is different things for different people), the Bible teaches us that we can coax these unwelcome behaviors into responding to the authority of God. Jesus shows us how to rid ourselves of damaging behavior in three easy steps. (Everything that Jesus did was to show us that we can do the same thing.) Read Mark 1: 25 and you will find that we have only to:

1. Rebuke the spirit. (Renounce the judgmental belief controlling us —refuse association with any sordid thoughts we may be harboring.)
2. Affirm peace. (Replace the imagination with some form of meditation or affirmation recitation that fills us with peace.)
3. Command the spirit to leave. (Tell the thoughts to go away—

speak forcibly out loud, if necessary. Our mind, which controls the decision making process of our body, can learn to obey our commands.)

Express your gratitude by staying close to God. (Luke 8 tells how several women who had been healed of unclean spirits and other infirmities stayed close to Jesus, providing for him. We can do the same by maintaining a deep prayer life and supporting the ministry of our choice.)

Though it may seem impossible when our child's inappropriate behavior claims the limelight, all those negative daydreams of sure disaster are now replaced with higher, more productive ones. We have learned that God wants our inner thoughts to be images of truth. Since truth is God and God is love, an obsession with issues of morality is best replaced with love. God wants our hearts to be full of mercy, and he wants our walk with him to be steadfast—not to be pulled off course by constantly thinking about the possibility of another person's "wrong doing." When we are able to stand humbly on the strength of love during tough moments, we have come to terms with the fact that we're not in control of our child's spirit. We can't make him be like us. We can't make him show a different face to the world. However, having freed ourselves from the burden of making moral judgments, we no longer feel the need to make assumptions. Instead, we choose to show our child the spirit of enlightenment and the mercy of God's love expressed through us, and in this moment, our role in God's plan becomes very clear, indeed.

He has showed you, O man, what is good.
And what does the Lord require of you?
To act justly, and to love mercy
and to walk humbly with your God.
Micah 6: 8

Pray With Me Now

Oh God,
I am so grateful for new insight

and
for a deeper understanding of your love.
Amen

Something to remember: It is not my place to fight my child's moral battles. That exciting privilege belongs to him, alone. Whew! What sweet peace.

CHAPTER 9

Choose Joy!

A PRAYER

Dear God,
Yesterday, I was certain that we had "rounded the corner"---that the problems
with our child were in the past. But today, we learn of more trouble, and I am
sad beyond words.
Why, God?
Why can't we have long-lasting joy like other parents?
Why does it always have to come to this?

What you want to know: Why is there no end to the problem? Why must my happiness always be squelched with sadness?

What you need to know: Emotional joy is never lasting----only very plentiful.

For the parents of troubled children, such joy seems to be particularly short lived. Perhaps a grown son has just landed a new job and is full of exciting plans for establishing a better, more productive life; or maybe our teenage daughter has broken up with a wayward boyfriend and is promising to come home earlier and attend to her studies. Maybe our household has such a lovely sense of calm, that we thought we'd made it "home free." At any rate, the house practically purrs with our happiness---for a short time. Then, as suddenly as the period of grace fell upon us, we are once again catapulted into the chaos of difficult parenting. Our child has done something surprisingly out of character for this stage of development. Or some authority figure lets us in on the fact that our child is not really succeeding in a certain area that we thought he was doing well in. The feelings we're now experiencing are those of disbelief, panic, anger and overwhelming sadness. But in the end, it is the sadness that takes command.

Watching a child fall backwards is like becoming wealthy and then suddenly losing all our money. We wish we'd never known how good it felt to have money because then being poor again wouldn't hurt so much. But many wealthy people make and lose several fortunes in a life time. They've discovered that even though wealth doesn't always last, they can return to their source again and again for another opportunity.

So it is with happiness. Emotional joy will probably not last indefinitely, but there is an everlasting source of supply. The problem comes in returning to this supply.

Maybe we've had so few moments of joy that we think we don't know how it works. (Disappointments can make the law of abundance seem rather farfetched.) Then, too, we may be so unaccustomed to feeling "up"; we're not even sure how we got there in the first place—much less how to return.

This is not where I tell you that Jesus wants you to "buck up" and try harder. On the contrary, this is where I let you know that the universe allows you to be sad. This painful passageway you are now in is simply another part of the journey through life. Read Job's wonderful story in your Bible. It will not be long before you see that lamenting his sorrow helped heal this man and left us with some beautiful, important portions of the Bible. His story reminds us that yes, sometimes God does permit all the seeming good in our life to be taken from us, and then, just when we see no justice in the situation, he gives us his love---which turns out to be greater than anything we've lost. Furthermore, it seems that in many of our favorite Bible stories, the message is that the more worldly processions or needs that we lose, the more supernatural gifts we receive---gifts of tolerance, love, peace, faith, hope, forgiveness and much more.

One way to help usher in joy is to practice the presence of God. This is because the presence of God manifests itself as peace and joy in our lives. Try simply being aware of God no matter what you're feeling at the moment, and recognizing the authority of God under all circumstances. Whatever is happening right now is according to his design. When we are in his presence, and not looking at things through the human perspective, we are acting from a place of love. We stop criticizing and complaining and start expressing gratitude for the very fact that we are in his presence.

Realize that it's not wrong to feel disappointment and sadness. Both of these emotions are just expressions of energy. Talk to your inner self. Tell it that you loved it when filled with joy, but that you also love it when sad. Spend time honoring that sadness. Retreat to your ark. Prayerfully send love to these sad feelings, asking God to replace this negative energy with positive energy. You will experience restoration in the pattern of daily living. Now you are feeling the undertow of events, but if you will relax and not fight against this difficult life current, you will find yourself riding back into the stream of life on the crest of a beautiful wave. It happens insidiously. As you float, looking for an opportunity of re-entry, your attention is captured by a new idea, an artistic project, a spiritual revelation, a new opportunity for service---it could be anything---but suddenly you are smiling again, and you know that joy has returned.

Pray With Me Now

Dear God
I long for lasting joy,
but
thank goodness
for your lasting love.
Amen

A good idea: When you are asking yourself why your child lost momentum, consider the answer. Difficult children have built a life around being different and unpleasant. They may be afraid to leave this comfortable, known way of life behind. They may also be afraid of being hurt at some point. As long as they are their "ol' selves," they don't have to worry about rejection and unkindness---it doesn't ever stop, so they don't know the difference. Perhaps they have developed a loser/loner lifestyle—messing up later might be more difficult on them than messing up now. If this sounds like your child, bless him with your belief that he will one day not mess up.

It might also help to examine the situation for clues to aid in the prevention of digression. Were we making our child defensive? Were we smothering him? Were we placing unrealistic expectations on him?

Another thing to consider is that sometimes there is a physical reason for regression. A diagnosis of diabetes or bi-polar are just some of the problems that could cause a person's behavior to change dramatically from one day to the next.

Even when the answers to these questions are not what we would wish for, this is a moment of truth to build on. This time period is a "jumping off" point in your life---a time to look at the situation honestly, appraise it and take new action. We are "jumping" in a different direction. This is not a time to drown in disappointment, but an opportunity to look at the "old" under new light.

> Those who sow in tears
> will reap with songs of joy.
> He who goes out weeping,
> carrying seed to sow,
> will return with songs of joy
> carrying sheaves with him.
> Psalms 126:5-6

A good idea: Try blessing everyday happenings---the sunrise, the sunset, television, washing machines, dryers—Bless the little things and you will remember to bless the bigger ones.

CHAPTER 10

Unwanted Gifts

A PRAYER

Dear Father,
No matter how hard I try, my child doesn't want my help.
And you know what?
A child's rejection is the ultimate rejection.
How am I supposed to feel?
Something other than helpless?

What you want to know: Why does my child reject my efforts to help him?

What you need to know: It's nothing personal.

Oh, yes, it is confusing when a child seemingly refuses everything we offer---our love---our financial resources—our culture. Sure, if we've "washed our hands" of him, the situation can be reckoned with, but when we've done nothing but try and try and try, the child's refusal of us is perplexing and painful.

"He doesn't let me help him with studies, but he consistently performs poorly at school."

"She won't wear clean clothes even though I wash whatever I find of hers that's strewn about the room."

"He won't eat meals at our house."

"She won't participate in family celebrations."

The questions of "why?" loom larger than life, but there's no easy explanation for this kind of behavior for those of us who grew up under traditional social rules. We simply can't understand such rejection in the face of love. Sometimes our pain is so severe, we consider emotionally withdrawing. The reason being that if we stop offering our love, we wouldn't have anything to be hurt over. At other times, we think if only we could know the cause of the rejection, we could continue as is, but with greater tolerance.

So, here is the good news. Your child's refusal to accept what you offer is not a matter of rejection. When it seems that the child doesn't appreciate your efforts, you may simply be giving more than he is capable of receiving at this time. No matter what we're offering, the other person has to be open to receiving. But our child isn't open, because even if it seems he hasn't learned very many rules of society, he has grasped this one very well. Receiving renders one obligated.

Even when we don't ask the child to do something or to behave in a certain way in order to receive our gift, most of us give with the hope that doing so will bring about a dreamed-for outcome. In other words, we haven't released our idea of shaping and controlling the child, and he knows this.

A gift, however, has to be fully released after it has been given. This means given with no thought as to what the other person will do with it, and with no thought as to how much it meant to us in terms of cost and effort. It isn't just "not expecting a thanks;" it's not thinking about the issue at all. Even thinking back with regrets about having given in the first place is a form of holding on. When a gift is not fully released as it is given, it isn't a gift at all.

Sometimes our gifts may seem to be less than welcome, because they are less than wonderful gifts. Think carefully about what it is you are offering, and try to interpret it through the mind of your child.

Is it transformation? There is often the deep-seated, if not outspoken, dream of completely transforming our child. If only we work hard enough and long enough, he will eventually change, we reason. He will become the person we want him to be. But even when our child acknowledges the need for change, the gift of transformation is not exactly ours to give. We cannot transform another person---we can only transform ourselves. Perhaps our child's disinterest in our efforts is because he innately knows this. Ironically, it is our own transformation that allows us to see the world through different eyes, making our child acceptable "as is."

Quite often, the offering of help we place in front of our child is in the guise of criticism. We think if we continuously "ride" him about all the things he's doing incorrectly, he's certain to benefit. This is a huge misnomer. To prove it, think back to the last time someone told you how to improve something by pointing out your errors, and you'll probably change your tune about helpful criticism. Interestingly enough, the most painful of these experiences usually occurred in childhood, when we weren't quite sure how we felt about ourselves. Having someone point out our faults most likely only underscored those already anemic feelings of self-worth.

Another gift we frequently want to bestow upon our children is our wisdom. We look at him standing in front of us—a baby to his parents at any age—and want him to benefit from our mistakes. We are so eager for him to be a success and are so full of wonderful ideas. Why shouldn't he be willing to take advice based on our lifetime of experience? But when our child turns his back on this advice only to have things turn out exactly as we predicted, what he's really saying is, "Let me live my life." You see, when we interfere with lessons the universe wants to teach, we stunt our child's growth. No wonder he backs off.

Still another unwanted gift that we frequently insist our child take is "shared misery." Worry and fear of consequences love company, and it's common to want our child to worry about his behavior as much as we do. For one thing, we may believe that we can scare him into right choices, but we may also just gain a sense of satisfaction knowing that he is at least a little worried about the outcome of his poor choices.

It's easy to see how these unwelcome gifts can be hidden within the beautiful, ornate "wrappings" of a family's culture, and cause the child to misinterpret our efforts. But it's not to say that we should stop making the effort. First of all, it may help to realize that in spite of old social beliefs, a gift doesn't have to put a person under obligation---even when the gift involves intangible things such as time, energy and emotions. A child will be quick to sense when a gift is truly given without expectations.

Secondly, consider revising your gift list. Try giving the kind of gifts that are not easily refused, because the recipient doesn't even have to be aware that you have given them.

➢ Give compassion.
➢ Give thoughts of peace.
➢ Give forgiveness.
➢ Give prayer.
➢ Give a good thought.
➢ Give silent praise.

There will, of course, be times that we have to make the physical effort, and these are the things we do without expecting a particular response. Listen when your child wants to talk, even when you don't want to hear what he says. Help out financially, even when you feel he doesn't deserve it. Remind him of family celebrations and set his place at the table, even if you know he won't be there. You are not helpless. You are in control—giving what you can and want to give. And if all of this sounds a little unfair in its one-sidedness, just remember that it is our Father's good pleasure to give us the kingdom---and yet, most of us turn our backs on the offer without ever thinking about what it could mean or how it could change our life. (So, maybe our child's behavior isn't as weird as we thought, uh?)

Pray With Me Now

Thank you God
For the gift of your love
that is always there,
even when I think I don't need it.
Amen

…for your Father has been pleased to give you the Kingdom.
Luke 12:32

CHAPTER 11

The Anger Storm

A PRAYER

Oh, God,
Forgive me.
But I am so angry right now.
And I am so sick of this child verbally abusing me.
Why is there so much anger in our home?
What does it take to bring about calm?
Please help me.
I can't take much more.

What you want to know: How did the anger between me and this child ever get started? How do I stop it?

What you need to know: Anger is not an unconquerable enemy.

Sometimes it's hard to say which is the more difficult situation to manage—your child's anger directed toward you or your own anger directed toward your child. But let's start with your child's anger toward you, because this is what usually precipitates your getting angry at him.

First of all, be assured that the torrent of ugly (perhaps even obscene) words shooting out of your child's mouth in your direction, are not as carefully aimed at your heart as you may have imagined. Anger is simply an energy storm—an uncontrolled rush of feelings expressed in a negative way, and there is probably a sensible, "no-fault" reason that it seems to erupt so often in your household. For one thing, these children usually have a metabolic explanation for their anger that may require medication. However, we often find that older or grown children don't take medication as they should, and furthermore, sometimes the medication isn't the right "fit." Certainly, such concerns should be taken to his physician, but keep in mind that although your troubled child may be diagnosed with a particular problem and is taking medication, he comes to you in anger from a place of emotional pain. In other words, there may not be a medication to take that pain away. This is a child who has painful experiences on a daily basis due to failures and who suffers the pain of taunting, ridicule and exclusion in almost every social encounter. Because his life experiences cause him to see things in an eschewed way, he may honestly believe you have caused the pain.

Try not to become defensive. All he really wants is your love. Lashing out with words of anger is the only way he knows to release his feelings of pain and the fear that you may not have enough love in your heart for him. It's just a primitive survival technique. Looked at in this way, you can see that even when there is the hidden agenda of blame, your child's anger is not personal.

Your silence at these times of your child's violent outburst helps restore balance to the atmosphere. You are not silent from weakness, but from love and understanding. Of course, sometimes, in spite of good intentions, we find ourselves yelling back, rather than being silent. Our emotions have slipped beyond their normal expression, because we have taken on the bad energy of the child and are releasing it in the easiest possible way.

It goes without saying that yelling back to the other person is not the best way to release bad energy. Instead, learn to recognize when you are taking on another person's mood and feelings. You will probably be able to realize that your mood was just fine before your interaction with the angry child. Often, just being aware of this is enough to calm your own energy by giving you a sense of control.

You can also stop an inappropriate reaction to anger by removing yourself from the presence of the child and taking a meditation break. Almost every aspect of meditation carries some degree of benefit for overcoming anger. The symbolic preparation of washing one's hands and drinking a glass of water, not only signifies your readiness to enter the silence, but actually helps cool the body heat produced by anger. Likewise, the deep, rhythmic breathing of meditation slows the heart and provides the overall sensation of relaxation.

Angry, adult children still living at home, challenge your patience in a different way. With less control over them in other areas of daily life, you enter their field of anger with the feeling of inadequacy. In this scenario, the best course of action may be to help them find another place to live. Talk with a professional counselor or search the Internet for organizations that can advise you on this type of action.

Sometimes we arrive at a place of anger by accident---when we don't know what else to do. We don't know how to react to our child's behavior or some item of information that's been shared. We know that what we say isn't going to help, but we say it anyway, and the tension turns to anger. Such anger is a type of miscommunication. In this instance, neither person sets out to hurt the other, but the words used to communicate don't say what we want them to. A feeling of helplessness becomes the driving force behind the yelling and screaming, and before long we have entered the storm head on. Again, saying nothing is usually the best course of action. It's fairly difficult to argue with silence. (Though, do understand that I'm not talking about the "refusal to speak" type of silence.) When our silence is sincere, and we're not *inwardly* angry, we place the matter in God's hands, where communication can take place in his way and in his time.

Regardless of what caused the anger and how we choose to handle it, however, it may help to remember that the physical body is only an expression of the spiritual and emotional nature. The spiritual nature is the real essence of the person and should be the leader, but obviously, our angry child has an overactive emotional nature and is allowing it to lead. *We* do the same thing when we react in anger. The child within is running wild---but it doesn't have to be destroyed, only purified and trained. We train by practicing self control---we purify by engaging in spiritual studies and by learning to look for the beauty of love in everyone and everything. Spiritual growth calls for us to learn to act from higher places than simple emotion, but it is not a growth process that must take place without help. All we need to learn about anger and how to overcome it can be found in the Bible.

Take the story of Moses. If you think God doesn't understand uncontrolled anger and the lack of development behind it, it's been a while since you read the story. Remember, Moses became angry when he saw an

Egyptian mistreat a slave, and consequently began beating the Egyptian. In fact, he grew so angry and lost such control that he actually ended up killing the Egyptian.

There is a lot to be learned from this incident. For one thing, anger sets boundaries for us. Moses didn't realize how deeply he felt about his people being enslaved. Killing the Egyptian was his moment of recognition. We often experience this kind of awakening when a child's behavior pushes us to extreme anger. Suddenly our boundaries of what we will accept and what we won't become very clear. Then too, every time we try to solve a problem by ourselves, instead of turning to God for help, we are metaphorically "killing our Egyptian," or falling short of God's expectations of us by reacting at a lower level than he would like us to. Isn't this what's happening when we get angry in response to our child's anger---trying to stop the problem with our emotional nature? Just as important, however, is the fact that Moses did gain self-control---eventually. He even went on to be used by God in spectacular ways. What a comfort to know that no matter what our child's anger has cost him or "us," others have gone this way before and come out okay---and in many instances, even better than okay.

Learning to act peacefully under trying circumstances is one of those lessons that may not be completely mastered in this lifetime, but we will want to make the effort, if for no other reason than the idea of building peace consciousness, for building the consciousness of world peace must surely begin at home when confronted with the little battles. And though we probably *could* just sit back and wait for the story to develop, as it did with Moses, we live in a spiritual era that equips us with all the right tools to make the learning process a little easier. This means that even when things don't go well between us and our child, and we're not exactly proud of our reaction to a situation, we can keep on going—keep on learning, knowing that we're one "goof-up" less toward restoring harmony and good will to our every day existence. We are learning to respond from a place called love.

Pray With Me Now

Father God
I am so grateful that you can take
our "not so good" moments

and
fill them with grace.
Thank you.
Amen

Thought for the day: Emotions can be felt and expressed as hate or love. Always choose love.

A good idea: Ask God to replace any negative energy you may be experiencing with positive energy. A few examples of positive energy could be:

<u>Thinking loving thoughts</u>. Visualize a heart encircling the person you're dealing with at a given moment. No matter what is being said to you, silently say to yourself, "I love you anyway."

<u>Being kind to everyone you encounter throughout the day</u>. Treat people as though they're special. Kindness can turn any potentially bad situation into good.

<u>Helping someone.</u> Open doors, pick up dropped items, etc… the positive energy at such moments is enormously refreshing.

<u>Singing.</u> Turn on the car radio and sing loudly. You'll reach your destination in high spirits.

<u>Smiling</u>. A smile says "I like you, it's okay, and you're in friendly company." It's an important way of letting people know that their encounter with you is going to be positive.

<u>Laughing</u>. Laughter is highly charged with positive energy. If there's nothing to laugh about, find it in a funny movie and allow yourself to escape in humor.

<u>Believing God's plan is a part of everything that is happening right now</u>. When we practice our faith by believing that we are currently in the right and perfect place and all is well, we fill the environment around us with positive energy.

CHAPTER 12

Word Power

A PRAYER

Dear Father,
How does a parent know what to say?
I need to give advice---don't I?
My criticism is needed---isn't it?
My cautions are important---aren't they?
But, somehow, instead of being helpful, my words become weapons in the fight against my child.
And it's then that I realize I shouldn't have said any of it.
So, how does one develop a controlled tongue, God?

What you want to know: Does what I say to my child really matter? Could I really make things worse by saying the wrong thing?

What you need to know: Well, yes.

Not to scare you, but words tend to have a life of their own and have been known to be quite powerful—especially when spoken. Maybe power is felt because it's our breath, so essential to life itself that provides the force behind the spoken word. At any rate, all of us living with an impulsive family member have not only experienced the sting of unfriendly words, but have fallen under their spell by responding in like fashion.

Hurtful words don't sound like anything that should ever be allowed, much less condoned, in a family, but when our child (regardless of his age) slashes out at us with insults, it's surprising how volatile even normally timid people can become. Home has suddenly become a battle field of words excused by the experts with the explanation of safety. We yell and make biting remarks at home, because this is where we *can* yell and *can* make biting remarks. This is where we can say anything and still be loved and forgiven. And yes, we do need a safe place, but not more than we need the truth of love.

Whenever love is truth, we know that whenever we're using hurtful words, we're losing our focus on truth and entering the world of half-truths. This is dangerous ground for strong relationships, much less fragile ones.

Hurtful words are words that:

belittle
throw a bad light on someone
show disrespect
stir up trouble
lie

At least one big blunder that we as parents make is assuming that what we say is always in the best interest of our child---because, after all, we love him. Our reasoning may go something like this:

If you really love someone, you point out the negative, even when it's damaging.

If you really love someone, you make sure he knows where he's wrong.

If you really love someone, you make certain he feels sorry for being the kind of person he is.

If you really love someone, you help him feel less about himself with humbling, character-building statements about his abilities and appearance.

If you really love someone, the truth is always best.

Of course, only the last statement is true. If you really love someone, the truth is always best, because the real truth is always love. What kinds of words express truth? Words that show:

respect
admiration

gratefulness
kindness
encouragement
forgiveness
honor
appreciation
recognition

You will probably be able to come up with a few more yourself. The key is to look for words that a loving relationship could be built on. Loving words are like holding someone in a warm embrace. They offer comfort and hope and affirm the other person as a child of God. Troubled children need to hear words of comfort and peace as much as the easily loved child

How do we know when a word is right? Sometimes it helps to ask yourself a simple question before speaking. Will what I say help—or just shut the child down? Whenever we do find ourselves criticizing (and we all will now and then), stop and send a bundle of love to the child. Visualize yourself taking him into your arms and comforting him as you would a small child. Then see your child in your mind's eye improving in whatever situation happens to be at stake at the moment.

Yes, words have power, but don't allow your child's angry words be more to you than words. Let the fleeting words of anger from your child go straight over your head. Even the worse combination of words such as "I hate you," and "I wish you would die," fail to carry the intended hurt, because you don't accept them. You don't let them enter your emotional space. Nor do you honor them with shock, anger or pain.

As your child matures, he will most likely begin to recognize his impulsive nature and actually regret it at times. You may be the recipient of a late night call explaining that he didn't really mean it, that he's sorry for what he said. And with this apology, you celebrate the new, wiser people you have both become. You give thanks to God for allowing you to align with light and order during a time of chaos.

A few practical guidelines:

1. Choose words carefully. Say exactly what you want to say---not necessarily what you feel.
2. Don't allow yourself to be emotionally misrepresented.

3. Don't make something big out of something little. This means don't embellish or exaggerate stories or events.
4. Practice using words in a positive way. Have stock answers for the more common questions. Here are a few examples of questions and answers.

<u>How do you feel about such and such?</u>
Possible answers:
"I'm excited."
"I'm totally committed."
"There is such clarity in our plan."
"Our resources are so abundant."

<u>What do you think of this person?</u>
Possible answers:
"She's so peaceful."
"He's so pleasant."
"She's genuine."
"He's a team player."

<u>How are you today?</u>
Possible answers:
"I'm excellent, thank you."
"I'm enthused!"
"I'm happy!"

<u>Need to give someone an encouraging word?</u> Try these statements.
"You're making progress."
"I'm proud of you."
"I can see how much you want it to happen."
"You have everything it takes to do this successfully."

See how good, positive, high-energy words sound? They uplift and inspire. They motivate and encourage. They literally make us believe the best about life. But if unkind words dominate your present vocabulary, don't despair. It's often easier to form new habits than to break old ones. Start with the goal of using words to describe the following feelings at least once during the day.

respect
admiration
gratefulness
kindness
encouragement
forgiveness
honor
appreciation
recognition

Here are a few examples:

Honor
"I'm proud of the way you did that."

Gratefulness
"I'm so glad we've had this opportunity to talk. I'm glad you're my child."

Forgiveness
"I'll always love you, no matter what."

Double the number of times you use the words each week. List types of words and statements made from them in a little book and mark them off (in private) as you make progress. It won't be long before you won't need a reminder or a gimmick to use positive words---they will have become a part of you and your new reality.

Pray With Me Now

Dear Heavenly Father
I rejoice that you are a teaching parent.
I shall be a learning child.
Amen

A practical hint: One very good way to keep only positive words between you and your child is to learn the art of light conversation. Talk about the same things with your child that you would talk about with a best friend; the movies, good books, pets and current events. Leave the controversial issues of his life alone.

The tongue has the power of life and death,
and those who love it will eat its fruit.
Proverbs 18: 21

CHAPTER 13

Could Badgering Count?

A PRAYER

Dear God
I am most certainly a
parenting failure
for
I give in to badgering again
and again.
Give me the strength to say no
and the wisdom to see the purpose in it.
Because people say it's best.
People say my child would have never gotten in trouble if I had been better at
saying
No.

> What you want to know: Am I the world's worst parent? (Or somewhere pretty close?)

> What you need to know: No. You are fairly average.

There is a saying, "get over it---you're not special." I don't like this statement, because I don't believe our God mass produces. We *are* special. However, I think this comment is surely meant for moments such as this, because whatever "this" may be, it is your life, and things happen in life---some of them are good---some of them are bad, but no one is singled out for bad. Look around you. More than likely you will be able to come up with several examples of people who have suffered through parenting trials just as traumatic as yours. Often these people are our contemporaries, sometimes they are prominent public figures and sometimes they are historical figures of another era whose real story only comes out through the revealing grace of time.

Perhaps some of the most startling examples of parenting difficulties can be found in the Bible, a book which many of us have been taught to associate with perfection. However, Bible characters may not always make the exemplary decision when the lesson is moving in a different direction. For instance, many parents in the Bible fall victim to the same types of issues facing us today---even badgering.

One such parent was Samuel; his children - the Israelites. For years, the Israelites had been governed by judges, and the system had served them well. So, as Samuel reached old age, he appointed his sons to step in and serve as judges for Israel, even though they were not as high principled as their father. The people, however, not only did not want the sons leading them, they wanted a king. They asked Samuel over and over for this, but he was against it because he knew exactly how it would turn out, with conscription, loss of personal liberty and heavy taxation being only the beginning. Unfortunately, his opinion meant nothing to the Israelites who continued to badger. Finally, Samuel gave in, giving them a King as well as a rather detailed list of how things could go wrong. And they did. Read about this in 1 Samuel 8-31. Things could have been easier for the Israelites had Samuel not given in---but they would not have learned the lesson God intended, and history might have taken a different course. So was it wrong of Samuel to give in?

Another example of such parenting difficulties is in the story of Samson. As mentioned elsewhere in this book, the Bible gives a pretty vivid picture of a spoiled, willful and disobedient child in Samson. When his parents tried to interest him in an appropriate marriage match amongst his own people, he would have nothing to do with it.

We can only imagine the screaming, yelling and crying that played out between him and his parents. In the end they gave in and soon found themselves at the wedding of Samson and a young woman from another tribe. This wedding ceremony was the beginning of the end, and who is to say how the story of this Bible giant would have ended had he obeyed his parents? But Samson and his life had a role to play in God's plan. Everything that happened in his life was a part of this plan. So was it wrong for his parents to give in?

These are wonderful Bible stories for struggling parents because they show us that our problems are not as unique as we often think. They also show us that there are no hard and fast rules when it comes to following God's direction. And finally, they show us that even if our action wasn't what would have been God's first choice, he will still be able to use it for the glory of his plan.

Sometimes we may indeed parent in ways that other people condemn or misunderstand. Sometimes we may not understand the actions we take ourselves. Does it matter? We know we should never agree to anything we're uncomfortable with or that we know is wrong for our child, but when the unthinkable does happen, and our parenting decisions seem to be momentarily falling through the cracks of sound thinking, perhaps this moment is a point in time that can only be played out by giving in to the presence of God. Perhaps we are living in a God moment; a moment that is part of a greater plan---God's plan. The good, the bad and the inability to fight off badgering is going to work out exactly as it is supposed to when Spirit is leading the way. Surely this is a long-ago truth made especially to comfort parents of the difficult- to- parent generation, and most certainly, it is a truth of love.

Pray With Me Now

Dear God
Thank you for enabling me to recognize my weaknesses,
yet still find and know your love, as well.
Amen

CHAPTER 14

What Now?

A PRAYER

I have just received the bad news.
I am devastated, Lord.
My world has collapsed.
Somehow I must gather the strength to face my child.
But what do I have to offer except
my anger,
my sadness,
and
my disappointment.
Again.

What you want to know: What can I do to help me through those first shocking moments of learning about my child's wrong-doing?

What you need to know: You have everything it takes to get through this moment with poise and a sense of style that expresses Christ's love.

Perhaps the most worrisome part of learning about our child's recent indiscretion is how to handle our immediate reaction to this information. We are understandably hurt, angry and scared. We may even be in a state of shock or denial, because even when dealing with a child who is habitually in trouble, there are still plenty of unpleasant surprises left.

It's in this "unstable" emotional condition that we must meet our crisis head on at the jail, in the principal's office, in a hospital's psychiatric wing or maybe just in our bedroom where we have been crying tears of grief. Our child sits across from us, not speaking—his arms crossed against his chest as a show of hostility. Perhaps we find ourselves swallowing back those first angry words that want so badly to come out and attack him. But even this restraint is not enough. Without these once depended upon word weapons, our feelings have no place to go.

Of course, we have been in this land before, so in a way, we are experienced pros—except that we don't want it to go the way it has in the past. We know if we react to this crisis like we have every other one, this time will simply be "another" time. But we don't really know what else to do. Right now, we are thinking that there is no choice but to feel the way we have always felt at such moments.

"You don't know how it feels," is a commonly uttered retort to well-meaning friends trying to lift our spirits.

The truth is, however, this moment can feel however we allow it to feel—even in a time of crisis. So, if we are looking for a more peaceful reaction to a situation, we must first find the presence of God within ourselves.

There is a well-loved affirmation that goes something like this:

Wherever I am, God is, and all is well.

When we say this, we know right away that everything is going to be all right, because we have touched base with God. God doesn't make bad children. In his eyes, our child is a divine creation. As we come face to face with this child under whatever circumstance, our job is to recognize his divine, spiritual nature.

Think about it. How would you approach a spiritual being in this situation? With anger? Resentment? Hostility? Probably not. Most likely, we would see the encounter as an opportunity to meet God, and this is exactly how we can find his presence in this moment. We can literally rearrange our thinking so that even during a crisis, we are able to approach our child as we would God—quietly, lovingly and respectfully. Here are a few of those new thoughts to help you along the way.

<u>Think well of the child</u>. Dig deep into the recesses of your mind and come up with good memories and things you like about him, so that you can think on these things, even during hard times.

Speak well of the child. You know God has a plan for your child. If this is the only positive thing you can say right now, it's enough.

Bless your child. There is the theory that some children arrive in the world with their parents' blessings, and others don't—depending on where the birth falls on the time line of the parents' career and emotional growth. If this child arrived at an inconvenient time and was not blessed with your welcoming love—change things now. Either verbally or in a written note, give your sincere blessing to him. A blessing can be stated any way you want. It's a statement of fact about the good that you know is within and about the child.

A few examples are:

- I love you and appreciate you.
- I behold and respect the Christ in you.
- You can be anything you want to be.
- God has a plan for you.
- You are precious to me and to God.
- You are God's wonderful gift to our family and we believe the best in you.

Praise the child often—if not in person, mentally. Many great things happen as a result of mental action. Praise him for making it this far without getting killed. Praise him for having nerves of steel. Praise him for being able to take whatever punishment is being mandated.

Turn gifts into hidden teaching opportunities for your child—faith builders for yourself. Gifts of money become "futures or life investments." Gifts of clothing become "image builders." Speaking of what you are doing for him in such high terms, gives importance to every little action.

Do these things even if the child is in jail and the future looks bleak. Remember that whatever happens—good or bad—happens to awaken us to God's love. And with every different moment being an opportunity to meet God, we know we can pass through this moment of sorrow with confidence that growth is on the other end of the moment.

Pray With Me Now

Father God
Thank you for giving me the ability
to meet this moment,
and for knowing that that is all I have to meet.
Amen

Thought for the day: Certain tigers and other dangerously wild animals are on the endangered species list, to be approached with care and respect. Above all, they are to be protected from predators. Wild animals are not more important nor more valuable to society than your wild child who is now (whether rightfully or wrongfully) being pursued by a predator of sorts---the legal system, the school district, unfriendly contemporaries, etc. Think of him as endangered—protect him with your love and prayers.

CHAPTER 15

Lonely Hearts

A PRAYER

Dear God,
My heart aches with loneliness,
for I have no friends.
None of the other mothers have ever wanted to be with me because of my child.
At first, it was because they were afraid of his influence upon their children.
Now, it's because they confuse my values with my child's recent actions.
So, I am alone,
tired,
depressed,
and sad.
Help!

What you want to know: How do I climb out of the valley of loneliness?

What you need to know: Loneliness is a state of mind that can always be overcome with effort and determination.

But should the effort even be made? Might loneliness merely be another form of misdirected energy that needs to be looked at from a different stance?

The loneliness of a broken-hearted mother is a sense of isolation that comes about because she believes no one understands her life. Actually, this is pretty much a true assumption. Few people do understand and appreciate the life and needs of a mother in crisis—particularly if her problem is a child who runs against the grain of society. People are afraid the child will be a bad influence on their children or even that the mother might not be of good character.

Sometimes the cause of our loneliness is more cleverly disguised. A child moves out of our immediate life because of choice or incarceration, and we are left with more time to face ourselves and contemplate the problem. We are not as busy as we were when the child's demanding life ordered our days. Now, the challenge of finding a new focus is vacant and lonely.

When the lonely mother does turn to books, church or family for advice on how to dig out of her hole, she is often met with the predictable.

"It takes being a friend to have a friend."
"Do something for others."
"Get out and mix."

What these well-intentioned people don't realize is that the lonely mother may not be able to follow this kind of advice, because she could very well be trapped by the negativity of the feeling. Loneliness is low level energy at its best—the kind that can literally sap strength and vitality out of a person. This is why it may appear that the lonely person doesn't want to help herself.

Loneliness doesn't lend itself to problem solving or solution seeking, but can be unmercifully powerful over its environment. If we allow it to have the upper hand, it will quickly build a wall between us and God's good. But, on the other hand, if we keep looking toward God even in the midst of our loneliness, we will see that good is always God's intent.

Beginning with the story of creation, the Bible shows us that good was the intent behind God's creation of the universe, and even though man didn't always live up to those good expectations, scripture continues with story after story of how God took a not so good situation and turned it into good. This is what stands before you right now—the challenge of a not good moment that you must turn into a time of high energy and right thinking. We do this by changing our perspective on loneliness. Instead of viewing this solitary time as a curse, we welcome it as our personal guide for the journey we are now on.

Finally, there is time to surrender to quiet and delve into self discovery. Yes, it would be pleasant to have people to talk to and do things with, but such activities are usually enjoyed at the price of never truly contemplating one's life situation. So, instead of a fun, exhilarating phase of life, you have been given time to restore yourself physically, mentally and spiritually. Whatever lies ahead, you are now awaiting restoration in the safety net of God's love. What an absolutely incredible gift from the one who loves you best. Reach out to accept it now, by first taking care of your physical needs.

> ➢ Rest. But take scheduled naps—no sleeping all day.
> ➢ Eat. But not frantically, or fitfully. Feed yourself healthy meals served on artfully arranged trays.
> ➢ Read. It doesn't have to be the Bible, but choose wisely so that the time will have been spent in an uplifting way.
> ➢ Exercise. There's no need to dread the challenge of getting in shape. Concentrate on the joy of moving your body by taking long, thought-provoking walks.
> ➢ Meditate. Learn if you don't know how---practice if you have already acquired the habit.

Allow yourself to make important self-discoveries. Find your balance. Find what is truly important to you. Find peace and how to become a complete person. Allow yourself to look within and determine what it is you believe in and what you hope for.

During this time in which God has not permitted other people to enter your life, look for his wisdom in the matter. While friends are undeniably a blessing, we do need a degree of inner strength to weather the demands of friendship, because friendship can be hurtful at a time when we are sensitive and vulnerable. For one thing, even good friends tend to want to talk about the bad in our life. (They think it helps.) Then, too, friends give advice that is usually unwanted. (They think we need it.) Not to mention, that the time friends take from our daily routine can prevent us from developing our life in ways that could truly help. If, for instance, the absence of a friend has enabled you to really pray and read your Bible, you can be certain that God is holding you in his protective hands of love. Settle down and enjoy his presence.

And if you can't feel God's presence right now—pray to feel it. Pray to be equipped to handle a friendship—to be full of smiles and to have a listening ear. Pray that someone else who is praying for friendship will be sent your way.

Pray With Me Now

Almighty God
Thank you for your patience with my child-like selfishness.
I accept your loving friendship
and will try
to make it enough for now.
Amen

Thought for the day: Whenever we are seeking a person to meet a need---rest assured that *that* someone is at this moment seeking our need to meet hers. It's just a matter of allowing God to put us together.

CHAPTER 16

Never Mind, God

A Prayer

God?
God?
God?
I---I
Oh, forget it.
I don't know what to say.

What you want to know: What's the best action to take when I'm feeling such despair that I literally can't make my heart form a prayer?

What you need to know: God, in his infinite wisdom, has already made arrangements for just such moments as this. It's called the Holy Spirit or Comforter.

When life is at its worst, God doesn't expect more than we can give. In fact, he has even anticipated our human frailty by providing something super human to step in and take over. The Holy Spirit is that vehicle for truth. Just what this is and how we obtain it is never easily or adequately explained. However, it is an inevitable bonus of being a Christian—any Christian. We own the gift regardless of whether or not we're associated with a "Spirit Filled" denomination or whether or not we speak in tongues. We continue to own it even when we fail to utilize or acknowledge its presence, but when we do decide to call forth and recognize the power of the Holy Spirit, we are overcome by the magnitude of its power.

Most people express the Spirit's presence as a sense of calm or a feeling of perfect peace. It's as if you are suddenly in the hands of an all-knowing counselor who is showing you exactly what you need to do to get through the trial, and you know from deep down inside that everything is going to be all right.

The outpouring of the Holy Spirit often comes to us through prayer. So, whenever you are feeling despair, ask a close friend to pray for you. This could be done over the telephone, if not in person, but ask them to pray for you there in that moment, so that you can hear the words. If there is no one whom you can ask to pray for you, open your Bible to John 17. Read the entire chapter. It is a prayer, and it is for you.

"My prayer is not for them alone. I pray also for those who will believe in me through their message, that all of them may be one, Father, just as you are in me and I am in you. May they also be in us so that the world may believe that you have sent me."

John 17:20-21

Can you make it through this moment? Yes---read John 17 and be reminded that Jesus is praying for you right now. He has given you his glory so that others through you will know the power of his father.

Do you have anyone to lean on? Yes---read John 17 and realize that Jesus is praying for you right now that you will discover the strength of unity that binds all of us who believe with the knowledge of God's love.

Be filled with his joy.

Be calmed with his protection.

Be strengthened by his glory.

Finally, be loved by the perfect love Jesus wants you to have. The last verse in this chapter tells us that Jesus understood the importance of our being loved.

"I have made you known to them, and will continue to make you known in order that the love you have for me may be in them and that I myself may be in them."

John 17:26

When you have read all of John 17, ending with the above verse, you will know without a doubt that your request, "Pray for me," has been answered in the real time of right now.

Pray With Me Now

Holy Spirit just breathe on me,
and I will know that you are with me.
Thank you
Amen

"But when he, the Spirit of truth, comes, he will guide you into all truth.."
John 16: 13a

CHAPTER 17

The Bad, the Good and the Great

A PRAYER

Oh, God,
My world is falling apart.
Nothing will ever be the same again.
What do I do now?

> What you want to know: Can this really be happening to me?

> What you need to know: Yes, and it's not all bad.

When it seems that your world is falling apart, you can be fairly certain that it's not an illusion. Your personal world of people, places, things and events is indeed falling into rubble at your feet. However, from the wiser perspective that you now have, you can enjoy a moment of elation, as you realize that finally, you are a part of the world at large—sharing in the forces of nature that bring about change. For this is the way the world morphs into being.

Think big. Earth plates move, breaking land apart, pushing oceans forward, and toppling structures both natural and man-made. Storms tear across the world, knocking down, covering up, and redesigning the landscape they travel over. Plagues erupt, pestilence multiplies, and living creatures fall and rise in the struggle for dominance. From moments such as these, we are given breathtaking sights such as the Grand Canyon, the Columbia River

Gorge, the Hawaiian Islands, flat plains, rolling hills and jagged mountains. Not to mention our own place in the scheme of God's plan.

Sometimes, it takes destruction to make the new occur in nature, and since growing up is a force of nature; it should come as no surprise that for some of us, the path to growth will be destruction of the old. We are at a place where only a complete change will help.

Our child has closed the door on what seemed a last opportunity for success.

Our child has made a poor decision and broken the link to the acquittal of a crime.

Our child has walked away from our efforts to help and our offering of love.

Whatever the results of these actions, we are left with the feeling that it's over—there is no hope for redemption on any level.

But take heart. A complete change is in the works. Right now! And just as we could never have dreamt of the Grand Canyon's magnificence, we cannot imagine what God has in store for this child. We can only accept the fact that all of us whose lives seem to have fallen apart are being reminded that we are in the process of an on-going rejuvenation of the mind, body and soul.

There is no need or benefit in trying to figure out the outcome of this moment. The moment is not what it appears to be. Analyzing it now is like looking at your reflection in the side of a car. The image you see is ugly and distorted, but it's not what you really look like. Nor is this moment what you think you see. No matter what it looks or feels like, God's love shows us different possibilities and asks us to wait patiently for the dramatic change to come.

We need not fear God's ability to handle "this one." He has experience in far greater scenarios than our little problem. He shaped the world from the chaos of swirling matter, and with each exciting change, pronounced the result as good. Of course, even if we were there in some un-molded form of energy, we didn't have to fret and worry about how the ocean and dry ground would turn out while it was in the making; nor did we have to fuss and fidget as he separated night and day and filled the earth with animals. In our uncreated state, we were completely trusting in the events that took place. Now we are a human being. Nevertheless, when it comes to creation and changing the face of things, God has not made new rules. He is still

God, and we are still his beloved. Whatever he does with the situation in front of us will be possibly dramatic and definitely good. It's an exciting event, and this time, we are a part of the process. No, nothing will ever be the same again. God's plan is to make it better.

Pray With Me Now

Dear God
Thank you for the creative force behind your love.
I look forward to the new.
Amen

An interesting thought: While we are not in charge, we *can* assist God in his creative work. Here's how.

1. Breathe. Breathe deeply, filling yourself with the life force of oxygen. Encourage your body to drink of its healing essence. Breathe comfortably, allowing yourself to feel the natural rhythm of the universe. Tell your body to move as it directs. Breathe slowly, focusing on the process that leads to relaxation and peace. Sink into this moment of bliss.
2. Listen. Listen attentively and hear the sounds of the universe. Listen for information to learn from. Listen for music to dance to. Listen for the voice of God and move to a world of higher thoughts.
3. Be. Practice emulating the great I Am. I am happy. I am well. I am at peace. I am loving. I am successful. I am satisfied. I am!
4. See. Envision good. Let your mind's eye see only that which can ultimately result in good. Nightmares and fears are not real, so don't allow your mind to even entertain these ideas on a fleeting basis. Command them out of your mind and replace them with a scene or thought of happiness.

An interesting truth statement: Everything visible was once an invisible thought.

CHAPTER 18

A New Story and it's Yours

A PRAYER

God,
I am not proud of the past.
Things didn't always go the way I wanted them to go with this child,
and I have bad memories.
Even when I know it wasn't my fault, I am still filled with sadness
that things couldn't have been different.
Ease my mind and calm my aching heart.

> What you are asking: Is there anything I can do to ease the pain of hurtful memories?

> What you need to know: There is nothing from the past too sacred to change.

Change the past? Is this possible? Well, why not? What is the past? Can you go back to it? Can you put your finger on it? Is it even real? These are the questions that prompt me to invite you to re-write the story of your life.

Begin with a time line marking the entrance of your child's presence in your life, and then make a notation of the significant events that have taken place throughout this time. At first sight, things might not look too pleasant, but in the realm of our greater perspective, we know that there is not just one right way for things to turn out. We will leave these incidents with God to utilize for the highest good.

Now, imagine meeting your child today for the first time. It's a fresh beginning of the mind, and you are intrigued with the spirit that God has placed in the body in front of you. You're so grateful to be a part of this new life about to unfold that giving thanks seems the most appropriate action to take. Like Hannah in the Bible, you have waited a long time for this moment, and so you follow her to the temple where she once dedicated her child to the Lord. You, too, will give this perfect human being back to God.

As you place his hand into that of the high priest and turn to go, you are saying farewell to much that you know and may even enjoy in its own macabre way. It's goodbye to the fear that you've held for the child's future, goodbye to society's expectations for him, goodbye to impossible family dynamics, goodbye to unhappy memories, goodbye to your old way of thinking.

The Bible tells us that Hannah visited her son on occasion, always bringing him a new robe to fit his growing body, but her role had been drastically changed. She had come to a place where her job was to watch and appreciate, while God did the rest. This is where you are today. Cover your child with a new robe of prayer and understanding. Then, give him a glance of loving approval. Finally, after many years of anxiety and heartbreak, your job is to simply sit back and watch God use his child.

Getting Started

Sometimes designing a new life story requires a clearing of the field before we can begin anew. One way to do this is by building a collage of our broken life. With pictures and various memorabilia, we depict our past life as broken into bits and pieces. Use a piece of stretched canvas as your working space and decoupage the items in place. The result could be truly impressive, but no one has to know why you made it or what it means. Only you need know that the symbolism in the collage lies in the brokenness of the elements. Everything in the picture is over. Shattered, so to speak. We will not try to reconstruct that life again. Now, we are free to start telling the true story of hope.

Looking Inward

It's time to make another time line, but this one must concentrate on you---not your child. Take one year at a time and write about the one thing that took you out of yourself and made you realize there was "more." You will soon find that you have developed a meaningful chronicle of events.

Our experiences have brought us to where we are one event at a time. In this passing of time, we have made a million decisions---some prayerfully---others quickly or impulsively. Maybe there are a few regrets in there, but fortunately, God transforms even those poor choices into useful lessons that can lead us to higher ground.

Notice your story sounds wiser and deeper in thought as it builds. This is the story of your spirit unfolding. Gradually, we see ourselves recognizing the right paths more often, and receiving more blessings than challenges. As you see this exciting transformation taking place in your own life, be aware that this "thickening of plot" will also occur in the life of your wayward child. It will change, because God is writing new chapters into his life even during difficult times.

Pray With Me Now

Thank you, God, for the possibility
of there being a new story for me and my child.
I am ready to turn the first page today.
Amen

Something to remember: Don't forget---your Savior is a resurrected Savior. Anything and everything in your life that has gone amiss can be resurrected and made new.

CHAPTER 19

Forgive and Really Forget?

A PRAYER

God,
He said it again.
"I'm sorry."
And I don't want to hear it
Because I don't believe it.
He says it over and over.
Day after day.
Year after year.
But it doesn't mean a thing
You said to forgive 70 times 7
Remember?
Well, I've been there and done that
And then some.
So, I want to know –
When do I get to stop forgiving?

> What you want to know: When do I give up on this thing called love?

> What you need to know: Never.

Somewhere on this journey of unconditional love, you will come face to face with forgiveness. Some of us forgive easily and are criticized for being pushovers. Others, who have perhaps reached their personal level of tolerance, will find forgiveness a road-block to happiness. And then, of course, there are those of us who vacillate between the two----loving and understanding on one hand, angry beyond forgiveness on the other.

It's more pleasant and maybe even easier having a forgiving spirit than to be a person who struggles with forgiveness-- unless you live with someone who views the forgiving nature as a weakness. But my real guess is that few of us are as truly forgiving as we think we are or as we appear to be. Here's why. When we truly forgive our child for his wrong doing, it means we forgive the child and the action. It means we let go of our anger and stand back to watch God. It isn't our forgiveness, or our child's forgiveness that's at work here. It's the forgiving love of God, directed through us. This thought enables us to look at particularly difficult-to-forgive acts with an interesting question: who are we to stand in God's way?

Our God is a God of compassion and definitely a believer in second and third chances. Grab a few well-known Bible stories from your memory and reflect on God's forgiveness and willingness to give another chance. Through Noah, the earth was given another opportunity to flourish, in spite of God's earlier decision to destroy it as a means of getting rid of wickedness. Jonah was given a second chance to serve God after absolutely refusing to do so earlier. Jesus gave Peter three tries to do the right thing and still loved him after he failed.

Need someone more realistic for company? If so, King David of Israel might just be the perfect soul mate for your spirit, for his story is a dramatic account of unconditional love. Though his son, Absalom, wasn't the only family member to disregard the rules of life, he was David's favorite child and was probably considered the most troublesome. A good-looking, popular, national idol sort of guy, Absalom used his influence with others to secretly plot a coup against his father. It was the ultimate betrayal and could only be met by David with a counter-attack.

But here is the interesting part of the story. As his troops left the city, King David gave these words of command: "Be careful not to harm the young man Absalom for my sake." Unfortunately, however, Absalom suffered a brutal death and David was heart-broken, wishing he could have been killed instead. Such love can only be known by parents of the most difficult children.

Was David an enabler in a dysfunctional family? Perhaps. Some Bible scholars do label him as an ineffective parent. But for those of us who recognize the feeling, it's more probable that David, like us, simply had a child his heart refused to give up on. Like other Biblical stories that teach forgiveness, David's story is a model of forgiveness based on love. It tells us loud and clear to go ahead and forgive again, and again and again, because there is never a reason not to love.

We forgive because we love. However, there is another side to the story of forgiveness that may not be as easy as forgiving our child. This is the forgiveness of the person who wronged our delicate, fragile child. It's often surprising how years after the fact; we can run into someone who mistreated our child and still be filled with feelings of anger and hatred. Why does something seemingly buried with time still hurt us so vividly? Because we have not truly forgiven. Now, we are not looking at the shortcomings of our child, but at our own failure to learn. Just as it will take our child a long time to learn the art of true apology, it may take us a lifetime to fully and freely forgive a person who has purposefully interfered with our efforts to train this child for his rightful place in the universe.

God's love is more powerful than anything human. Mistakes, wrong thoughts, unkind words and evil deeds can all be erased with it. We don't have to do anything to accomplish this erasure; we just have to make sure that the incidents requiring the erasure aren't ruling our life with displaced power. This is how we can suddenly realize that some dark incident of the past doesn't really bother us anymore. We have put the issue so far out of our mind, that when it does push itself forward, our new awareness doesn't even recognize it.

Instead of spending time praying for someone to change or to see his "wrong doing," in its proper light, all we really need to pray for is that we will begin to see what happened with different eyes. We don't ever have to be best friends with the people we have had issues with, (and, in truth, we probably won't be), but we can be given the ability to see these people in a new light. They were put in our path for some kind of lesson or test. Poor things, if they failed it, they will have to take it over again somewhere else down the road.

It's never our job, and completely unnecessary to punish people for unkindness. I've discovered the universe works very much like the ocean. Whatever we throw into it comes back like so much flotsam on a wave of energy. But it doesn't always come back to the exact point of release, and it is sometimes drastically changed for the worse. By the time nature returns the goods we've thrown into the ocean, for instance, wood has usually become blackened and gnarled, shells are often crumbled into slivers, and bottles have broken into pieces. Not to mention that the scavenged treasure we pick up may have been put into the water a few continents away. Unkind action has similar ways of returning maybe close, or maybe far from where it was thrown out, but not necessarily to the perpetrator, and with damaging action much worse than anything we witnessed earlier. If you ever stand back and watch this natural occurrence, you will probably stop seeking revenge, because you will want nothing to do with its unpredictable nature. Likewise, there's no point in trying to explain this phenomena to the person whom you view as the perpetrator of unkindness. It would probably not make sense to him, and it serves no part in the act of forgiveness.

True forgiveness is cleansing. When we have forgiven, there's no need to point out faults or to criticize a particular action. Being critical of the past action is counterproductive to the healing process. Instead, we want to clear the air with positive energy which in turn cleans the slate.

Still finding the idea of total forgiveness without criticism a little hard to digest? Then, think on this. Would you refuse to forgive or stop criticizing while standing on holy ground? Probably not. But if God is everywhere and always with us, aren't we always standing on holy ground?

And so it is. The universe of everyday life is made holy and sacred because of our belief in an omnipotent God. How wonderful that after every ugly act we take part in as humans, we can become new and perfect beings bound in a relationship of love made possible by God's gift of forgiveness. How wonderful to be made in his image and have it all.

Pray With Me Now

Dear God
I ask your forgiveness
because I realize that I have been blocking the process.
I hand this situation to you and allow you to act
through me.
And all is well.
Amen

Little Tips To Help the Forgiveness Process

1. Don't think about the incident. Keep your mind on other things. Think about something that makes you feel good like puppies or kittens, and plant this visual image in your mind when tempted to dwell on the grievance. What we don't think about tends to become softened with time.

2. Give the other person an honest break. How would you really have acted under similar circumstances? Or, give the other person credit for what caused them to have acted inappropriately.

3. Realize that you wouldn't hold a mentally disabled person accountable for hurting you; nor do you have to hold the person under discussion responsible for your hurt. Mentally, emotionally and spiritually healthy people don't hurt others. Acting responsibly calls for clear thinking.

4. Learn to look at unkind people as you would an animal. Envision this person who has hurt you with whiskers. Would you expect a cat with claws not to use them now and then? Most likely you would excuse a scratch with the comment of, "Well, he didn't know any better, he's just a cat." The same type of thinking can be used as a catalyst for forgiveness. Realize this person who misbehaved so badly didn't know any better. He was acting as best he could for his level of human development.

5. Finally, know with confidence that whatever happened to have upset you so badly has very little to do with you and everything to do with a breakdown between that person and God. Regardless of how much we may want to judge, it's not our place.

Food for thought: Forgiveness means giving up something—giving up something such as a grudge or an anger that we hold passionately to our heart. When we forgive ourselves, we stop doing harmful things to ourselves such as blaming or reliving the scene. If we forgive our child for something we don't approve of, we give up our disapproval and judgment. This can be a truth moment that leads to freedom.

CHAPTER 20

What's Left to Do?

A Prayer

God,
Haven't I done everything you told me to?
Haven't I shown my willingness to forgive?
Haven't I shown my willingness to love?
Haven't I shown my wiliness to give?
But it's not working, God.
And
I really don't know what's left to do.

What you want to know: When one has done everything they know to do, what's the next step?

What you need to know: There's always something else to do in the cause of recovering a child.

What indeed should be our stance when we've literally done everything we know to do for our child as responsible and loving parents? Where can we go for help when we've practically been the experts on the matter at hand? Now, dear friends is the time for expansion—expansion of your love, expansion of your resources, expansion of your hopes and get ready for this one---expansion of your spiritual beliefs.

Not all problems are the same or of the same intensity. Some require more work than others. Jesus said that. When the disciples were unable to heal a boy, yet Jesus could, they wanted to know why.

"This kind can come out only by prayer," he told them. (Mark 9:29)

So, okay, but we have prayed. And prayed. And prayed. How could we pray anymore? By just doing it---making more time in the day to stop and actually put breath behind the words. It's a fact that few of us can actually claim having ever put enough muscle behind our spiritual life. Maybe all that's needed is a little more time. Then, too, there is the matter of doing things differently. Isn't that what this book is all about?

There are so many ways to pray; we know that, but most of us fall back on the format we're most familiar with. It's comfortable and in its own way—reassuring. But if we're not getting results, perhaps this situation is calling for a combination of prayer techniques. Now is the time to explore these different methods in search of one that more perfectly suits our needs.

The Written Prayer

If you live in a busy household or work in a public environment, you may not be praying as often as you'd like simply because there isn't enough private time in your day to say a prayer. Writing out our prayers gives us greater access to them. We can sit in a noisy restaurant, a crowded airport terminal, or right smack in the middle of our family life and be talking to God. You will be amazed at how effective this type of prayer is. In fact, many women returning to their past prayer journals for a quick re-read say they see evidence of divine communion with God.

"The words were so beautiful and looked so carefully crafted, I couldn't believe I had written them," one woman said in explanation.

Give written prayers a chance, particularly if you don't journal. Not only do you receive the benefit of deep, personal communication with God, but you are left with a record of life events.

The Affirmation X 15

Closely related to the written prayer is a written affirmation. This is a positive statement depicting success. It should be written 15 times every day until a feeling of release comes to you. It's a good tool to use when you just really don't want to pray anymore or when you don't know what to pray for anymore. It's easy, helps focus your emotions, and provides a positive space for your mind to be in for a few minutes every day.

Example: My child seeks high-minded, goal-oriented friends, and these people seek him as well.

The Angel Letter

There's never a reason not to turn to the angels for help, not even if you're an unwavering traditionalist. The Bible speaks freely about the existence of and the help God's people received from angels. We are no better than the people written about in the Bible, why shouldn't we need these beings' offerings of help, too?

A letter to an angel is short and to the point, because it, too, should be written 15 times, although it isn't necessary to do this exercise every day.

One does not have to be in a meditative state or make any kind of special connection before writing this letter. Our angels are with us all the time--- they'll find our message without any trouble. Your letter can be something like this:

To the angel of <u>your child's name</u>,
Please help <u>your child's name</u> to _____.
Thank you so much. I appreciate your help.
Your name

The Treasure Map

Most people know what a treasure map is---the poster style affirmation chart that shows cut-out pictures of what you desire, along with the written affirmation for each desire. The problem is that while we may have made one a long time ago, it has possibly been a while—a long while. Have you made one recently for your child and this particular issue at hand? Put your actions behind your know-how and do it. Treasure maps are wonderful reminder tools. Placed in a prominent place, it's hard to overlook them. Put yours in front of the television and promise yourself to read each statement before tuning into entertainment. A few of your treasure map affirmations might read like this:

My child seeks spiritual guidance and finds inner peace.
My child's current legal problem has been solved. The outcome is positive.
My child's future is bright as he now develops God-given talents and abilities.

The Prayer Group

Getting together with friends to discuss problems and pray for one another isn't necessarily a new idea—but your ingenuity can make it as "new" as you like. You could get together to discuss the book, *A Course in Miracles* or to build a Master Mind program. You could join an A.R.E. group (Association for Research and Enlightenment, Inc.) You could form a Bible study group that studies only scripture about Bible Parents. You could call your group a meditation group and ask everyone to go into their meditation with the energy of the group's hurting loved ones held next to their heart. Maybe just joining a new church will give you the enthusiasm to keep on with your quest.

Whatever you choose, just know that participating in anything new and different will introduce you to new thoughts and ideas for continuing to "fight the good fight," despite no current success. It's like a wave of fresh energy, itself. And who knows, one of these organizations or activities just might be the avenue leading to your success. You will find plenty of helpful information regarding the mentioned organizations on line. Forming your own group for Bible study or meditation only requires your desire and creativity.

Courses

When we're trying to make headway with a problem and just can't seem to do it on our own, it may be worthwhile to take a professional course in the area of our need. This could cover a wide range of topics---life coaching, relaxation techniques, developing psychic abilities, problem solving, etc. So, if you want to learn how to pray effectively, take a class. It's that simple. Prayer doesn't have to be a mystery—an out-of-control throw it to the wind and just hope sort of thing. You can learn or re-learn how to talk to God.

There is a plethora of prayer classes in every religion and venue one could want. Churches regularly offer courses on this topic. But pay attention to what's going on in your life---if you're not getting results from your prayers, it may be time to try new techniques. The Rev. Chris Chenoweth, who so graciously endorsed this book, teaches an excellent course on prayer and offers it in churches across the country for a love offering. In his classes you will learn to:

put God first
forget the past
stop negative chatter
dream big
live a steadfast life
accept God's abundance
and so much more....

Reverend Chenoweth also provides personal prayer, a free newsletter of daily prayer, a wide selection of prayer CDs and fabulous recreation opportunities.

However, if your image of prayer continues to conjure images of little old ladies wrapped in shawls, you may want to go an entirely different route. You may choose the world of science. That's right. The world of science is taking many people to their inner sanctum for answers and peace. One group doing this is Silva International, another organization whose president has generously endorsed this book. Certified Silva Method instructors will equip you with resources and teach you methods to:

develop a healthy belief system
use both sides of the brain
solve problems
heal yourself and others
control areas of your life you never dreamed possible
and so much more—all scientifically proven and all within your
personal spiritual guidelines

Never think you've done all you can do. When you're feeling discouraged, go to your ark, refresh yourself, regroup and get back on your feet. This is a story of victory and you have every tool to succeed.

Pray With Me Now

Dear God,
I thank you for your gift
of unlimited ideas. I know

Jayne Garrison

that as long as I am willing to
reach out for the new and untried,
my role in this miracle is still
viable—and I don't have to give up.
Amen

CHAPTER 21

The End of the Story

A PRAYER

Father God,
There is something I want to know.
It's not much, really.
I'm not asking who was there before you
or
how you got there in the first place.
I'm not asking how Adam and Eve suddenly had
friends for their children to marry
or
how Noah really gathered all the animals onto the ark.
I'm not asking what the Trinity looks like.
I'm not asking how it is that Jesus rose from the dead.
And even though, I'd like to know, this time, I'm not even asking what
happened to the dinosaurs.
But there's something I've got to know.
Something that I'm scared to know.
Something that is important to know.
Tell me Heavenly Father, how will it all turn out?
What will the end result be?
There are lives riding on the outcome, you know.

What you are asking: Will everything eventually be all right? Or not?

> What you need to know: God's plan is perfect. There are no bad endings to the story of our lives which, by the way, are always written by God.

It's normal to look at our child and his problems with questions about the future. The questions vary depending upon our formal religious training. For instance, for some there is the question, "Will my child behave once he is a baptized believer, joined a church, or become enlightened with truth?" The answer? Yes, your child will most certainly behave after being baptized or joining a church or after being introduced to truth principles, but it may not always be in an exemplary fashion. Then there is the question that parents of adolescents ask. "Will my child be more responsible as an adult?" Again, he will probably be more responsible in some areas of life, though it may not be in those that are important to you. And, of course, there is always the wish for an all-over complete change. "Will my child change by a certain time? The answer: don't we all change over a period of time?

So, you can see that any question about the future of our child is ambiguous and better left unasked. We don't know what the future holds for our child, but on the upside, we don't have to know. We are not in control. Even when we don't officially acknowledge it, God is the mastermind behind his own creation.

Uncertain beginnings are no cause for despair. Tiny seeds become glorious plants. Giant corporations often start off as floundering small businesses. Craft projects sometimes have to be started over and over before we're satisfied with the finished product. Bedraggled, stray animals often become beautiful, star quality pets after months of good care and nutrition. You can probably remember many such times in your own life when the end result surpassed your wildest dreams, because you did what you could and allowed God to do the rest.

Jesus gave us his life as the supreme example of this attitude, and when we follow him and place our child's future in God's hands, there are no risks and no surprises—we know the outcome is going to be good. God is completely dependable, because he can't be changed. When Jesus, hanging on the cross, placed his spirit in God's hands, he was living in a moment of crisis. Death was impending, and things couldn't have looked much worse.

But, by placing his spirit in God's hands at this moment, Jesus taught us some important things. 1.) God is the answer to everything—even in the most difficult situations. 2.) God is the meaning behind everything—even our lives. 3.) God is the only fate for a believing child—even if the child has had a challenging behavior problem. There is proof of this in the Bible. Read the complete crucifixion story in Luke 23, paying particular attention to the story of the criminals in verses 32-43. 4.) God is good even when it doesn't make sense to us that he should be.

Of course, while you and I can make progress with another person, we can't presume a "complete fix" or even assign deadlines for recovery. Only God working through and with our child can determine when the restoration that we long for will be completed. The complete healing of our child could occur after our earthly life—or even after the child's earthly life. We may realize only a portion of our goal for now, but this doesn't mean we have failed. Many lofty goals aren't fully realized in one lifetime. Think of people who spend their life working toward the elimination of world hunger or cancer. We would never think of judging them harshly or unfairly simply because the goal wasn't met in their lifetime. Rather, we admire such people for having been strong fighters for a worthy cause. So it is with you and me. Regardless of how visible or invisible our efforts, we don't ever have to give up. We can pursue our goal with dedication and enthusiasm for as long as we live—knowing that someday there will be a God-ordained, happy ending to our child's story.

Pray With Me Now

Dear Father
Thank you for this beginning
and
for helping me see that it is just that—
only the beginning.
I am grateful for your enduring love
that is not afraid of the unlovely.
Amen

Thought for the day: Don't be afraid of uncertain beginnings. Jesus was born in a stable.

CHAPTER 22

Postscript to Sorrow

ADDENDUM PRAYER OF SORROW

God,
They tell me that you were there
at the end.
So, what was this all about?
My prayers
My struggles
My hope
My dreams
The life now gone
out of all of them.
Was it a waste?

What you want to know: Was this life for naught?

What you need to know: Certainly not. No matter what the final outcome of your child's life appears to be, only God knows the end of the story, and God is love. Remember that and hold on to it.

There is nothing more tragic to a parent than losing a child. Particularly poignant are those situations in which the choice of a child's lifestyle leads to death. But let me remind you that death is not the only way we may lose these dear children. Some of our troubled children leave home and never come back. Others join groups of people that more or less separate them from us forever. Some end up with life sentences in prison, and still others simply choose not to meet us half way with efforts of reconciliation. The loss is a tragedy no matter how it comes about, and we are likely to feel ourselves drowning in sorrow at such times. It is a double sorrow of loss and sense of failure.

It may help to realize that not every relationship is intended to last a lifetime. There were wonderful friends (both children and adults) in our childhood whom we literally left back in time. There are fellow colleagues who moved on with their careers. There are businesses, whose presence grounded us in daily life, that have closed. There are entire communities that we have left as we moved up our own ladder of success. And of course, there are people who have died, leaving us behind to feel the emptiness of the place they once filled. This feeling of emptiness is what you are feeling when it appears that the battle with your child is over. Reflect on these other times when you were left, and know that you will survive this time as well.

Reread the chapter asking the question, "Is this my fault?" You took God's challenge and fought the good fight. You learned particular lessons designed just for you. You did what you were supposed to do with your life. And yet, you still hurt for the actions of your child. The unbelievable. The sordid. The unspeakable. The unforgivable.

Stop right there. There is no need to re-judge this life or action over and over. Be assured that whatever your child's battle was, it was not shocking to your heavenly father. In fact, your child's struggle with his highest good is the oldest story on the face of this earth. So, you do not have to go before God with a sense of embarrassment, you only have to go before him with thanksgiving for his love. The fact that we can appear to have failed so miserably in managing our lives and yet still deserve God's love is the beautiful story of everyone's life. The discovery of this truth may even be the entire purpose of everyone's life. Does any human being ever truly live up to his God-given potential?

If there was ever a time to read the Bible, this end-of-the-road scenario is an excellent time to take the Bible into your hands and look at it with the new insight you now have. What you will discover is that God's love is wider and deeper than we were ever taught as children in our Sunday school class. Follow me now, through just a few highlights of my own self-made discoveries.

In the beginning, Adam and Eve ate of the forbidden fruit and were thrust out of the Garden of Eden. One of the outcomes of this new knowledge was that they saw themselves as naked and were embarrassed. We heard this story as children and learned that there is punishment for our "sins," but what we may not have noticed is that God still loved this man and woman. No, he didn't undo the consequences—they never re-entered the Garden of Eden, but he made clothes for them to wear. Imagine a God so loving even at a moment of wrong-doing that he would bother with something as trivial as clothing.

Years passed. Adam and Eve had the children, Cain and Abel of whom little is known except for the gifts they presented to God. Abel gave the first born of his flock; Cain gave some of his crop, and God accepted Abel's gift, but rejected Cain's on the basis of his poor attitude. Cain was so jealous of Abel that he killed him and was condemned by God to live as a nomad. For all of our lives, most of us have carried in our mind's eye a mental picture of beautiful Able with a lamb in his arms. We never gave a second thought to Cain, who was depicted to us as wicked and punished for his "sins," and yet there is far more to the story than our Sunday lessons told.

Reading on, we find Cain crying out to God. He is claiming that his punishment is unbearable, for not only is he now relegated to a life of continual wandering, but he knows everyone will be out to kill him. God gently tells him this is not so, that in fact, if anyone kills Cain, that person will suffer seven times over. Then, God puts a special mark of protection on Cain so that no one *can* kill him. Yes, the consequence was not removed; Cain had to leave the comfort of home, but it was not without God's help. Imagine a God so loving that he would protect a man who had committed murder.

The next leading Bible giant we encounter is Noah, a man of such pristine character, God instructed him to build an ark and then helped fill it with animals so that when the bad people were destroyed in the flood, a few good people and a pair of each animal would be salvaged. We grew up admiring the image of a white-haired man reaching his arm out to retrieve a dove. Noah was a man to model one's life after. It was easy for us to deduce that when one is good, he will be saved, but if one is bad, he will perish. However, we didn't read it all. Later on, this grand old man was sleeping off a drunk when his youngest son found him laying there in the nude and disrespected him in some way that is not clear. Noah became so angry that he cursed his grandson. The whole scene from the drunken grandfather to the actual cursing of his descendentis a rather bad ending to a previously glorious story. And yet the Bible says Noah lived 950 years. Imagine a God so loving that he would allow an indiscretion without comment.

Soon, Abraham and Sarah are filling the pages with tales of intrigue. When godly Abraham is mildly threatened by a Pharaoh, it's no problem; Abraham simply gives him his wife under the pretense that she is really his sister. In Sunday school classes we were led to believe that before this relationship could be consummated, Pharaoh gave Sarah back because everyone in the palace was sick, presumably an illness brought on by God. Read between the lines of this story and make up your own mind as to what this illness might have been. "But the Lord inflicted serious disease on Pharaoh and his household because of Abram's wife Sarai." (Genesis 12:17)

Pharaoh says, "What have you done to me? Why didn't you tell me she was your wife? Why did you say, She is my sister, so that I took her to be my wife?" (Genesis 12:18)

Luckily, Abraham and Sarah continued their life journey without injury, but they still hadn't learned the lesson. They did the same thing with a king further down the road of experience, (Genesis 20) but this time God intervened before damage could be done. Again, as interesting as the story is, there is much left to the imagination. Don't bother. Instead, imagine a God who overlooks one lie after another and allows the liar to prosper and live a happy, full life.

Of course, there was the little matter of Ishmael, born to Abraham by his mistress. Dare we admit that here was a person predestined to live a life of difficulty? "He will be a wild donkey of a man; his hand will be against everyone and everyone's hand against him, and he will live in hostility toward all his brothers." (Genesis 16:12) The only thing we know for sure about his behavior is that he mocked Isaac at his weaning feast, and Abraham was forced to send him and his mother away. They fled to the dessert where God promised to look after Ishmael and make him a nation. It's kind of a story about not being the "special" one, and if you can almost hear the prophecy being whispered to you about your own child, or hear him taunting his brothers and sisters in like fashion, take note that the Bible says God was with Ishmael as he grew up and he took a wife from Egypt. He had many sons and lived to be 137 years old. Imagine a God who has good in mind even for those born to be mean.

We are not even out of the book of Genesis at this point, but I'm sure you get the gist of the idea. Historically, God has seen it all and still loved, which means that no matter what thing you have encountered with your child, there need be no shame or embarrassment on your part at the feet of God. Our God is a god of love.

There is one more issue that may be bothering you right now. Perhaps you are afraid that your child has left this earth without knowing God. If this is your concern, remember that we don't always know what goes on within another person. Since the body is only a house for the soul, perhaps the body's actions don't always represent the intent of the soul. Assume that in some split second before crossing over, your child's soul reached out to God. If you can't allow yourself this thought, then accept the fact that while theology professors may have figured a lot out for us, there is no one alive who has died and come back to tell us how it really is. I dare think most people will be very surprised to discover just how loving God is at the time of death. But since it is all speculation, cling to the one thing you do know, which is that your loved one was a part of something you couldn't understand. Even if the life and downfall of your child seemed only to serve the purpose of awakening others and showing them another way, this is something you can be proud to have taken part in. He served a purpose.

Endings are always sad because they tell us that one phase of life is over. Even when the ending is because the problem was cleared by some positive means, and we are no longer living in confusion, there is likely to be an element of loss. We want things and people to be the same—even if having them that way was miserable for us. This is a normal reaction to change, because the known is just more comfortable for us than the unknown. For those of us who have learned to look at the world with new vision, however, an end began the day we started to perceive things differently.

In the beginning there was God.
In every ending there is God.
Everything is okay.
Everything was okay.
We just didn't know it.
Now we do.
THANK YOU, MOTHER FATHER GOD

The P. S. I Love You Section

Extra Goodies to Help You on Your Way

To Journal or Not

People in crisis fall into one of two categories. They either record with a passion or they absolutely refuse to have anything to do with it. For the first group, journaling helps uncover fears, interpret dreams and even provide solutions to the problem. Keeping a daily record is a part of their personal healing. But the second group of people feels that recording negative events somehow accentuates them—makes them more real and formidable. They have a point. Not recognizing bad events with our memory, makes them become smaller and less important.

However, should you belong to this second group, take a moment to reconsider. Periods of distress often come with unusual understanding and insights. Dreams, conversations that we are either a part of or simply overhear, things that we read or divine ideas that seem to fall upon us from nowhere can come to us during these times with lightening speed and interestingly enough, disappear just as quickly. Some of these insights are profoundly revealing, and you will want to return to them for deeper exploration.

Following are journal pages that encourage you to record a simple thought, perhaps leading back to an even greater one at least once a month. Have fun with these pages, being sure to stretch beyond them whenever the situation or mood calls for it.

January

You can begin anew regardless of what lies behind you. Write an imaginary letter to you and your spouse discussing the changes you want to make in the year ahead.

February

The month of love. What better time to design a Valentine for your child. Nothing fancy. Just draw the outline of a heart and fill it with words that express your love, concerns and hopes and dreams for this dear one. It doesn't matter whether it's ever sent or not. The vibrations of your love as you complete the exercise will travel into the ether and find your child wherever he is.

March

March is that getting tired of winter month. Make a list of things you'd like to do and places you'd like to go. Remember, life doesn't stop for you just because your child is in a bind. Very often, it's important for him to see that you are continuing to live.

April

April might just be the month you choose for spring cleaning. Name five things in your life you'd like to get rid of. Discuss how you plan on doing this.

May

Here is a jubilant, happy kind of month—unless you faithfully follow the newspaper pictures of graduating seniors and feel remorse about your own child's lack of success. This month write about this sense of loss or some other negative feeling. When completed, tear the page out of the book and throw it away.

June

In summer, we sometimes feel ourselves drifting. Choose an affirmation for a matter of grave concern. Write it 15 times.

July

While you're celebrating your country's independence, why not celebrate your own independence from fear and anxiety? List your old fears and talk about how good it feels to be free of them.

August

The dog days of August. Decide not to be pulled into depression by heat. Think of five ways you can help keep other people cool. Write about your experiences.

September

The second new start of the year. Thank goodness for ample opportunity. What do you hope for yourself? Your child?

October

Sometimes the effort to keep going is so hard, that the greatest accomplishment we can make is to simply drink eight glasses of water per day. Remember, that whatever you've done to demonstrate success, is success. Write about one thing you've done this month. Just one.

November

Thanksgiving anyone? What better time to begin that gratitude journal you've been promising yourself to start. Practice getting the hang of it on this page. Name the people in your family who are there for you. Name your pets. List the items in your refrigerator.

December

Dare to be brave and unusual during this difficult time of life---choose to celebrate and do it with love. Give gifts that no one else will think of, like prayer and goodwill.

Just This Moment

A Guided Soul Play Meditation for You and Your Child

How to use a written meditation: Put soft, meditative music in your CD player. Read the meditation out loud several times. Complete the breathing exercise, close your eyes and visualize the scenes you have just read out loud. At first, it will probably not be exactly as read, but you will surprise yourself at how well you do connect with the scene. Don't struggle with it. If you can't visualize anything, just keep your eyes closed and listen to the music. Another option would be to record your reading of the meditation and use it to guide your consciousness through the exercise.

Inhale—exhale—inhale—exhale. Do this several times to equal counts without pause or holding of breath.

Welcome to this moment of your life.
No matter what has been or perhaps is still perceived as going on in your life—this moment will be perfect.
Look now at the situation between you and your child and realize it has no bearing on this moment.
Visualize your child's soul as a beautiful array of colors and make this statement:
"At this moment my child seeks the company of high-minded people and high-minded people are attracted to my child for this moment.
For this moment."
Now visualize the colors of your own soul—pink—blue—red—allow your heart to choose and send it forth to join the soul of your troubled child. See his own magnificent array of color beauty. You notice that no matter what

may have been going on on the earth plane, it is not occurring here. Your child's soul is happy, at peace, and beautiful. Most important, he is happy to see you, and your colorful energies begin to blend in love. Watch these energies become one---pull away and dance around each other---swirling---floating.

There will be no need to speak—not even in your mind. The soul has its own ways of communicating. You and your child are happy for this moment.

Now call forth the soul of the child's father (or mother). Envision the three splashes of color—meeting—blending—breaking apart—forming a circle and dancing.

For this moment the three of you are forming your spiritual family, and all is well.

Call forth the soul of your child's siblings. Welcome their splashes of color by absorbing them into the already blended three. Call forth the souls of spouses and grandchildren. Whoever needs to come into this circle should be asked to join. Take them into the arena of expanding reds, violets, blues, oranges, greens. Come together as one giant ball of soul energy—roll, bounce, feel yourself being tossed high into the atmosphere and coming apart into millions of tiny particles.

For this moment only, your entire family is an expression of pure love and joy for one another. Feel the bliss as the ball of energy reforms into cohesiveness.

Your play time has been perfect. It is only for the moment, but you know it is always there for whichever moment is at hand.

Knowing this, send everyone home and, hug yourself as you welcome your soul back to its earthly home.

Breathe deeply. Feel your feet on the ground. Open your eyes.

What To Do If Your Child Is In Trouble

1. Breathe deeply. Take a moment to realize that no matter how severe the situation appears, God is with you in this moment, just as he was before you learned about the problem.

2. Don't panic. Decide to follow a logical sequence of actions. Many of these bad events occur in the middle of the night. You can wait until morning to begin taking care of the necessary obligations or you can get up and handle business. Bail bond services are usually available 24 hours.

3. If your child has been arrested, look in the phone book and select a bail bond company. If the bail is affordable, you definitely want to get your child out of the negativity. However, if the bail is exorbitant (and they can be for surprising offenses), you should know that often, time spent in jail while waiting to go to court will count as "time served." Waiting for one's trial can be a lengthy, drawn out process. If your loved one doesn't have a job and is likely to receive a sentence of incarceration, you might consider earning "time" a worthy use of these months. Not to mention the fact that the money spent on bail could be used on a lawyer. At any rate, whether or not to bail your child out is a decision you can make with your lawyer, which is the next step on your list.

4. Contact a lawyer. Be aware that if the problem occurs on the weekend, chances are that no matter what the phone ad claims, you won't get past a recorded message. Be patient, Monday will arrive. If this is a first offense, it won't matter terribly whom you select, but if you're the parent of a repeat offender, you want the best you can afford. This is no time to give a "new comer"

a chance. Nor is it necessary to stick with someone you are unsatisfied with.

5. Retrieve your child from the jail. He will come to you as soon as he is released. You will probably not even have to go inside the facility, because the bail bondsman will tell him that you're waiting in your car. Have a cool drink and a light snack such as a sandwich with you. Chances are good that your child is thirsty and hungry, and food is a comforting white flag to wave.

6. If there was an impounded car, pick it up now. The car has probably already been searched, but just on the slightest chance that something has been missed, you want the vehicle back in your possession as soon as possible.

7. If your child was unfairly arrested or unfairly treated, have him write out the circumstances, then go with him to the internal affairs department of the jail and file a formal complaint. This should be done immediately. Contact the ACLU with your story. Every story helps the organization improve things for all people, but understand that they may not take a personal interest in your particular story. In other words, don't expect them to pick up your case for their next battle.

Other problems.......

1. If your child thinks she is pregnant, get a reliable, lab-performed pregnancy test before coming to conclusions. If the test is positive, there are many options, but wait at least one full month before deciding upon any of them.

2. If you've discovered your child is involved in drug use, seek help. Unfortunately, the smaller the town you live in, the less affordable, available help you'll find nearby. However, NA (Narcotics Anonymous) and AA (Alcoholics Anonymous)

have helped many people put their lives back together after addiction and has a presence in almost every locality. Take drug use seriously. It's not just a phase.

Emergency Information for the Mom or Dad of a Troubled Child

1. Put the telephone number of a bails bond service on your cell phone.

2. Always keep a high credit line on at least one card that could be used for bail or a lawyer.

3. Put the telephone number of a trusted lawyer on your cell phone.

4. Consider subscribing to law insurance.

5. Don't forget that time really is on your side. No matter what actually happens, you and your child will be all right because of the fact that you've chosen love, and in the end—the very, very end-- love is all that matters.

Statement of Gratitude

I am grateful to have been raised a Christian by parents who taught me not only to respect and honor other faith traditions, but to draw from their strengths and wisdom when needed. I am grateful for a husband who has loved me and been easy to live with for many years. I am grateful for my two beautiful daughters, the one son-in-law, three enchanting granddaughters and other family members yet to enter my life. I am grateful to have a comfortable house, good food to eat and clean water to drink. I am grateful for the opportunity to share this book with people who may benefit from it and for all the people who have helped me put it together.

Blessings and love to everyone who turns these pages in search of peace.

Jayne

Jayne Garrison is the author of five books, three of which were internationally distributed, including the popular, *Living With the Challenging Child*. Other previously published works are numerous magazine articles, fiction and non-fiction, advertising copy, corporate communications, a well-loved weekly newspaper column, "The Bayou Journal," and an informative newsletter for the parents of children with Attention Deficit Disorders, "The ADDvantage." A wife, mother and grandmother, Jayne is most happy when writing words of encouragement. She lives in deep East Texas with her physician husband and three strong-willed cats.